Society and Family Strategy

Society and Family Strategy

Erie County, New York, 1850–1920

MARK J. STERN

State University of New York Press

Published by
State University of New York Press, Albany
© 1987 State University of New York

For information, address State University of New York
Press, State University Plaza, Albany, N.Y., 12246

Library of Congress Cataloging in Publication Data

Stern, Mark J.
  Society and family strategy.

  Includes index.
  1. Fertility, Human—New York (State)—Erie County—
History—19th century. 2. Fertility Human—New York-
(State)—Erie County—History—20th century. 3. Family—
New York (State)—Erie County—History—19th century.
4. Family—New York (State)—Erie County—History—
20th century. 5. Erie County (N.Y.)—Population—
History. 6. Erie County (N.Y.)—Social conditions.
I. Title.
HB935.N7S74 1987   304.6'34'0974796   86-23121
ISBN 0-88706-495-7
ISBN 0-88706-496-5 (pbk.)

In memory of my parents

Contents

Tables

Figures

Acknowledgements

THIS study began in 1976 as a graduate research assistantship. In the intervening decade, I have acquired a mountain of intellectual debts that I can only begin to acknowledge.

The research for this study was funded by a grant from the Rockefeller and Ford Foundations' joint program on population and development. The University of Pennsylvania faculty fellowship program provided summer support. Finally, a draft was completed at the Center for Advanced Study in the Behavioral Sciences as part of a SSRC summer institute on Social Change and Individual Development.

A number of individuals helped me with the technical and methodological problems I encountered: Mirka Ondracek, Jeff Seaman, Gretchen Condran, and Michael Haines. For comments on all or part of the manuscript, I thank Bruce Bellingham, Michael Frisch, Susan Watkins, Mike Ornstein, Harvey Graff, Mike Doucet, Robert Cuff, Susan Houston, Edward Shorter, David Hogan, Ian Davey, Miriam Cohen, Olivier Zunz, George Alter, Hal Barron, and a number of anonymous readers for State University of New York Press. Shonnie Finnegan provided important assistance in locating sources in Buffalo. Robert Kilduff kindly shared with me his research findings on Buffalo philanthropy.

Charles Tilly twice read the entire manuscript and gave me helpful comments and advice. Michele Martin, my editor at SUNY Press, should receive combat pay for escorting this manuscript through to publication.

Michael Katz was the advisor for this study when it was a dissertation and has read more drafts than he probably cared to. In twelve years of working with Michael, he has never been at a loss for insight, suggestions, and encouragement.

Susan Seifert has had to live with this manuscript and its author. It has interrupted her sleep, her morning coffee, and her access to the word processor. Whatever is good in it owes much to her.

Introduction

HAVING children is a serious business. While it is left to individual couples to make the decision in our society, in the past, fertility was often regulated in direct ways by others.

And why shouldn't it be? Fertility affects the number of workers. It affects the number of children whom we have to educate. It eventually affects how many old people we need to care for and how many of us there will be to take care of them. Indeed, no baby boomer could discount the impact of fertility on social life.

Of course, fertility was never *just* a social decision, as the town elders in early modern Germany discovered when they restricted marriage and found themselves overwhelmed with bastards. Fertility is a personal decision that is tied to the most intimate elements of emotional life.

In spite of this, the explanations of the fertility decline have confined themselves to narrow paths. On the one hand, demographers have examined fertility as a macrosocial phenomenon—what they call "the demographic transition." Fertility changes are part of the general process of modernization. On the other hand, economists have analyzed fertility at the microsocial level—as a consumption decision by individual couples. From this perspective, having children is like buying a television set, albeit one that costs one hundred thousand dollars to maintain.

Several years ago, a demographer, commenting on the fertility debate, noted that economics was "all about how people make choices," while sociology was concerned with "how they have no choices to make." Rarely has a quip so accurately captured the gaps in a field.[1]

1

In the past few years, this situation has changed. A new generation of demographic theorists—unhappy with the vague generalities of modernization theory and the narrowness of economic explanation—have looked at those structures that mediate between the society at large and the individual family.

John Caldwell, Ron Lesthaeghe, John Knodel, and Etienne van de Walle have examined the role of socialization, family morality, and culture in the timing and pace of fertility decline. They have substituted historical research for abstract theory and have brought texture and detail to our knowledge of the fertility transition.

American historical demography has for the most part labored within the rickety structure of the older scholarship. Some scholars have been frustrated trying to operationalize the arcane variables of economic theory, while others have found themselves adrift in the generalizations of modernization theory.

One of the problems of American studies has been their research design. National studies mix apples and oranges, since different areas have different populations, occupational structures, and cultural compositions. Studies based on aggregate data make it impossible to disentangle the complex of factors—occupation, age, migration history, and ethnicity—which affected fertility. Finally, studies need a long enough time period to identify the various stages of the fertility transition.

The research project on which this study is based corrected these problems. It recorded information on over one hundred and fifty thousand individuals in one community over a period of sixty years. This allowed me to capture details of community and individual life that were often obscured in previous studies. I have combined this methodological advantage with the conceptual insights of the new demographic history to tell a different story. What are its main themes?

The fertility decline can best be understood by examining the intermediate structures of society—those that lie between "society" and the "individual." These structures—family, social class, and ethnic group—provide the workshops in which "society" is experienced by individuals and in which they try to make sense of it. I focus on three phenomena that have received a lot of attention in social history, but little in historical demography: the labor market and the opportunity structure, the interaction of social class and ethnicity, and the impact of education.

In the late nineteenth century, an organizational revolution swept the North American economy. The corporation became the common form of business organization and came to control a larger part of economic activity.

This managerial revolution transformed American social class and the labor market. A new social stratum of professionals and business employees—what I call "the new business class"—which had hardly existed earlier, became an important social group. At the same time, manual workers, whose workplace conditions had been converging, were split into two strata—those in the primary and those in the secondary labor markets, which drastically altered their material circumstances and opportunities.

The family economy of these new social categories was different from that of older groups. The new business class, with no property to inherit or to live on in old age, adopted new strategies for prospering, which included low fertility and prolonged education. By the middle of the nineteenth century, their distinctive family strategy was obvious.

Later in the century, the material circumstances of manual workers also changed. The misery of poverty, which had restricted choice and planning for generations, declined for those well-off workers in the primary labor market. Combined with changes in the opportunity structure, prosperity encouraged them to restrict fertility and send their children to school longer.

Changes in the class structure interacted with ethnicity. At midcentury, the United States was an immigrant nation, but one dominated by northern and western Europeans. By the beginning of the twentieth century, the "new" immigrants—especially Poles, Russians, and Italians—had arrived. While some immigrants came with skills or capital, most entered the lowest rungs of the occupational ladder.

Yet ethnicity qualified the character of their low occupational status. Some ethnic groups had enough skills to move quickly into better jobs. Others adopted strategies for "making it" in America. Finally, some saw themselves as temporary Americans, bent on returning home. Each of these groups read the American opportunity structure in a radically different way.

The "objective" opportunities were only there for those who saw them. Those immigrants who were either better located or bent on making it, moved rapidly to lower their fertility in the early twentieth century, while those who had fewer opportunities or were not interested in staying in America did not. The logic of lower fertility only made sense for some.

Education was the switching station for the change in family strategy. Prolonged education served as a means of realizing the new opportunities of the economic order. Invariably, those families who lowered their fertility also sent their children to school more.

I am interested not only in the whys of the fertility decline, but the hows as well. The general decline of fertility in the West is one of the major social changes of the period. In 1850, most European and American couples assumed they would have large families. By 1920, they assumed they would have few children. If we can gain some insight into how this change happened, it will help us to understand the general nature of social and cultural change.

This study addresses two issues. First, was the fertility decline a complete break with older family patterns, or was it a gradual process of evolution? Second, how do we explain the timing of the change? Was it the result of "utility maximization," as the economists would have us believe, or was some other standard used?

Some demographers, like E. A. Wrigley, believe that most families throughout modern history have known how to limit fertility, but began to do so more in the last century. Others, like Knodel and van de Walle, assert that the idea of fertility control was alien to earlier generations and that the fertility decline represented a new *mentalité*. The choice is between two models of social change. One model sees change as a gradual process of evolution. The other sees it as discontinuous, what Anthony Wallace has called a "paradigmatic process."[2]

The evolutionary model of fertility change is, in part, an optical illusion, the result of bad data. The process through which fertility declined was discontinuous—in the jargon of social science, a step function. If we disaggregate our data, we find that individual families and groups moved rapidly to replace one strategy with another. The illusion of gradual change is the result of using aggregate data that hide the complexity of the individuals' behavior.

When did change occur? Did individual families sit down every night, calculate the cost and benefits of one strategy and another and then make their decision based on maximum utility? No. As long as older strategies made sense, more or less, they were not abandoned. It was only when an older strategy stopped working that it was replaced. Viability, not optimal utility, was the standard of change.

In *The People of Hamilton*, Michael Katz noted that his method was one of "hard data and rash speculation."[3] The same could be said of the present study. The census data that is the backbone of this book provide us with reliable evidence on the size, composition, and structure of family life. It does not, however, tell us the motives, thoughts, and emotions of the women and men who participated in this momentous alteration of everyday life.

I have rushed into the breach with a set of systematic speculations on how and why fertility declined. Without them, in my view, this would be an incomplete story, and history is, after all, a discipline of stories. This may be wrong. But if my story encourages others to come up with their own stories—ones more consistent with the evidence—I will be satisfied with having stimulated their better efforts.

Fertility is a tremendously complex topic. My study is limited to just one community, it is limited by the available data, and it is limited by the scholarly resources of its author. Yet I hope it makes at least a modest contribution to our understanding of the decline of fertility and the larger social processes of which it was a part.

1

Explaining the Decline in Fertility

THE birth rate of whites in the United States declined by almost forty percent between 1855 and 1915. This reduction altered the structure of social and cultural life and the organization of the economy. It stands as one of the great social changes of North American history.

Many observers have considered rapid population growth in the lower classes and developing nations a major concern of our times. Yet, from the perspective of world history, this concern is ethnocentric. As Margaret Mead reminded us: "Each human society is faced with not one population problem but with two: how to beget and rear enough children and how not to beget and rear too many."[1] Even today, in developing nations, many families see underpopulation, not overpopulation, as the problem.[2]

This concern for underpopulation is not limited to the developing world. The "European marriage pattern" of late marriage, high mortality, and high celibacy maintained a rough demographic balance through the eighteenth century.[3] Still, the average peasant couple could look forward to only five or ten years of marriage before death struck one of them.[4] Even in Western society, then, the spectre of depopulation was more common than the fear of overpopulation.

The English and French colonies of North America were a great exception to this rule. According to Phillip Greven, the early settlers of New England were blessed with extremely high fertility.[5] In Quebec at the same time, married women gave birth to an average of eight children.[6]

The combination of low mortality, vast expanses of land, and high

marriage rates that produced these high fertility rates continued throughout the eighteenth century. In spite of the large immigration of the century,
the Colonial population was substantially native-born as early as 1660
and continued to be so throughout the early Republic.[7]

According to the Federal Census, there were 1.4 children under the
age of five for every woman in 1810. In the next generation, however,
fertility fell precipitously. By 1840, well before industrialization and urbanization had become generally felt, this index of fertility had declined to
1.1 children per woman, a fall of twenty percent in one generation. This
decline continued; in 1855, the native white birth rate was 42.8; by 1915
it had fallen forty percent, to 26.2.[8]

In international perspective, the speed and magnitude of the decline
in American fertility were exceptional. In 1830, the birth rate in the United
States was at least twenty percent higher than that in Western Europe.
By the early twentieth century, it was lower than those of England and
Wales, Austria, Italy, and Spain, and only slightly higher than Sweden.
In a matter of seventy years, the United States had become a low-fertility
society.[9]

Most scholars have focused on the rapid decline of the early nineteenth century. At first, the decline was attributed to industrialization and
urbanization.[10] But this argument was undercut by the lack of industrialization during this early period and the widespread reduction of fertility
in the even less industrialized countryside. If the decline of American
fertility were to be explained, scholars would have to study rural
populations.

Yasukichi Yasuba accomplished this with his study of interstate
fertility differentials.[11] According to Yasuba, fertility was higher in states
where it was easier to obtain new land, and lower were land was scarce.
Yasuba established the "land-availability" thesis as the central theory of
American historical demography.

Scholars have questioned Yasuba's methods and his failure to identify the links between land availability and fertility. Colin Forster and
G. S. L. Tucker confirmed Yasuba's findings, although they improved on
his methods by using multivariate statistics and smaller units of analysis.
Other studies, from New York to Indiana, have supported the land-
availability thesis, with only a few exceptions.[12]

In the late 1970s, Richard Easterlin, George Alter, and Gretchen
Condran used a sample of rural households in 1860 to examine more
precisely how the availability of land affected families' fertility.[13] Dividing

the households into five groups based on recency and extent of settlement, the authors found frontier families had lower fertility than families living just behind the frontier. Married women in older agricultural regions had the lowest fertility. As Easterlin noted: "It . . . appears that Eastern wives not only started their childbearing later, but terminated it earlier, presumably at least for some wives, by the deliberate limitation of fertility."[14]

Easterlin, Alter, and Condran were more successful at rejecting explanations of the fertility decline than in formulating their own theory. Their data did not support the link between fertility decline and higher dependency ratios of more developed areas, differences in education, differences in the opportunity costs of child-rearing for women, or land tenancy.

In the end, the authors hesitantly embraced the land-availability thesis. Easterlin speculated that the link between land availability and the decline in fertility was the parents' wish to settle their children on land near them, a point supported by Greven's study of Andover.[15] Although their data provided no ready test of this hypothesis, Easterlin, Alter, and Condran focused on the essential problem of demographic history: how do macro-social forces affect the micro-level decisions of individual couples?

Maris Vinovskis has raised the most lively and consistent dissent to the land-availability thesis. Vinovskis added other socioeconomic data to Yasuba's original data and used multivariate statistics to demonstrate that land availability was not a significant determinant when other factors are controlled. In a study of Massachusetts in 1860, Vinovskis found that literacy was a stronger correlate of low fertility than land scarcity.[16]

Vinovskis believes that fertility declined in response to the modernization of American society, the result of "broad shifts in attitudes and values throughout society."[17] A number of factors—increased education, the availability of information, the occupational structure, the perception of the individual's role in society, and attitudes toward children—contributed to a major attitudinal shift in the population. Unfortunately, as Vinovskis admits, his aggregate data do not allow him to test this speculative hypothesis.

Vinovskis's work marked a departure in American historical demography. The theoretical cul-de-sac of the land-availability thesis gave way to an interest in the broader changes in American society. By examining continuities in the fertility experience of the town and the country, Vinovskis made the problems of American demographic explanation more consistent with those in other areas of the world.

Two important consequences—one of substance and one of method—flow from this perspective. Increasingly in the past decade, American scholars have returned to how industrialization and urbanization influenced fertility in the last half of the nineteenth century. In addition, the problems of aggregate data have led to more use of nominal-level data.

In recent years, studies of American fertility have focused increasingly on the late nineteenth and early twentieth centuries. These studies share a number of features. They have used nominal-level data derived from federal or state manuscript censuses. They have chosen to describe trends and differentials in census populations, rather than to model or test causal explanations. While we have gained a much better sense of the contours of fertility in nineteenth-century America, our ability to explain these patterns has not improved to the same degree.

Vinovskis and Tamara Hareven's studies of differential fertility in Boston and a number of New England towns in 1880 found that ethnicity was the most important determinant of fertility.[18] In Boston, foreign-born women's fertility was 64 percent higher than that of native-born women. While the trends were more erratic in the small towns, there too ethnicity was the strongest correlate of fertility.

By contrast, occupation was only weakly related to fertility. Using a three-category measure of occupational status (high, middle, and low), Hareven and Vinovskis found that in some towns, the lowest occupational group had the highest fertility, while in others, the middle or high occupational stratum did. These inconsistent findings, the authors concluded, resulted from the complexity of urbanization in the nineteenth century. "Even within the same city," they note, "population groups behaved differently in different neighborhoods."[19] Hareven and Vinvoskis believed that no broad generalizations could capture the complexity of the fertility decline.

These provocative New England studies present a number of problems of measurement and categorization. They were based on a total of three thousand households. When these data were broken down by location, age, and the other variables, cell frequencies of only twenty or thirty were common. Thus, a high degree of sampling error is present in the estimates.

Hareven and Vinovskis's occupational classification, too, is questionable. It is not based on any theory of social class, and it is only a rough measure of occupational stratification. They may have failed to find significant occupational differentials in fertility because they used a poor measure.[20]

While Hareven and Vinovskis's work suffered because of its small sample size, Stewart Tolnay, Avery Guest, and Stephen Graham's recent work had the opposite problem: too large of an area. Based on the public-use sample of the 1900 census, their data corroborate the general pace and magnitude of fertility decline estimated by Coale and Zelnick. In addition, they found strong ethnic differences in fertility. Native white fertility declined sharply over the last one and a half decades of the 19th century, while foreign-born fertility showed no clear trend. By 1900, native-born white couples were clearly practicing family limitation within marriage.[21]

The national sample was less useful in establishing reasons for the decline in fertility. Levels of education, income, and manufacturing productivity were correlated with native white fertility. But with no way of taking social context into account, the authors could not explain these relationships.[22]

An alternative to the single case study or broad national methods used by these studies is Michael Haines's multiple case study approach.[23] Haines studied the fertility of miners and heavy-industry workers in an international perspective. Drawing on aggregate data from Britain and Prussia and nominal-level data from the Pennsylvania anthracite coal region and several communities in England and Wales, Haines discovered a consistent pattern.

> The conditions of work and the relative goegraphical and social isolation of mining and some industrial populations acted to preserve relatively high fertility norms characteristic of the semirural environment itself or at least to retard changes in tastes resulting from generalized "modernization" of attitudes toward reproduction. Given tastes and norms as relatively constant or changing more slowly than for the overall population, early income potential, relatively high wages, restricted female employment outside the home, possible secondary employment in agriculture or handicrafts, possible child labor, and higher mortality and debility would all have favored higher fertility and, in part, earlier marriage. Those factors would then have been combined with the peculiar circumstances of each individual situation, such as ethnic, racial, or religious composition, degree of urbanization, and level of education or literacy, to produce the final pattern.[24]

Haines's study demonstrates the wisdom of a modest strategy in studying fertility. Rather than explaining everything everywhere, he restricted himself to one particular population—mining and heavy industry—and studied the many determinants of its fertility strategy.

Although his findings are not readily transferable to the more variegated occupational structures of major cities or regions, they demonstrate that some systematic explanations are possible.

Scholars of North American fertility have met with success and failure. They have gained a better sense of the overall trends and the complex differentials in fertility. Yet, with the exception of the land-availability thesis, they have not explained the observed patterns.

Explanations of the Fertility Transition

Much of American historians' failure to explain the decline in fertility can be blamed on the weakness of demographic theory. Demographers have been more interested in measuring and explaining fertility in the modern world than in developing historical explanations. When they turned to the past, they searched for parallels between the West of the eighteenth century and the Third World of the twentieth, hoping to discover the "threshold" of development that would automatically set off the decline in fertility. The two major theories of fertility decline were the theory of the demographic transition and the economic theory of fertility.

The theory of the demographic transition asserts that the decline of fertility is part of the general process of modernization: when societies industrialize, urbanize, and secularize, the decline of fertility naturally follows. As Frank Notestein, the formulator of the theory, noted:

> The new ideal of the small family rose typically in the urban industrial society. It is impossible to be precise about the various causal factors, but apparently many were important. Urban life stripped the family of many functions in production, consumption, recreation, and education. In factory employment, the individual stood on his own accomplishments. The new mobility of young people and the anonymity of city life reduced the pressures toward traditional behaviour exerted by the family and community. In a period of rapidly developing technology, new skills were needed, and new opportunities for individual advancement arose. Education and a rational point of view became increasingly important. As a consequence of the cost of child-rearing, possibilities for economic contributions by children declined.[25]

The theory of the demographic transition really is not a theory at all, but a loose grouping of descriptive statements. It is appealing because it ties fertility to the major social changes of the past two centuries. It does so, however, by sacrificing clarity. What causes what?

The European Fertility Project, under the direction of Ansley Coale, set out to answer this question through the intensive historical analysis of regional fertility patterns. After a series of national studies, however, it found no "threshold" of modernization nor any stable pattern of social and economic correlates. The transition, Haines concluded, "is really a collection of variant patterns of fertility and nuptuality changes, and the relationships between demographic and socioeconomic variables are not constant or even very predictable in shape or magnitude."[26]

The theory lost prestige, as well, because of the baby boom of the 1940s and 1950s. The demographic transition was supposed to be an *irreversible* process, caused by a change in consciousness. Could it be that it was a simple economic decision, influenced by the changing costs and benefits of children?

Economists believed it was. For them, fertility is one of a number of investment decisions individual couples make. During the past century, the shifting costs and benefits of children led couples to choose to substitute fewer "high-quality" for many "low-quality" children. For the economists, the fertility decline was a simple story of couples maximizing utility in a world of changing costs and constraints.[27]

Historians had little use for the economic theory of fertility. The most thorough attempt to test it found its variables difficult to operationalize. Furthermore, the theory did not predict the actual patterns of differential fertility in nineteenth-century America. Rather than "reason out solutions from abstract principles and current stimuli alone," Peter Lindert concluded that couples, "economize on information costs by reverting to familiar paths. . . . They retain . . . patterns of preference, the roots of which extend further back than their personal memory."[28]

Economic and demographic theory both failed to predict the fertility history of the West. The demographic transition could not distinguish the causes from the consequences of modernization and oversimplified the process. The economic theory could not be operationalized and made predictions that were wrong.

In the wake of these theories' failure, a new generation of scholars attacked the history of fertility. John Caldwell, Ron Lesthaeghe, John Knodel, and Etienne van de Walle rejected the narrow cost/benefit logic of the economists but were more open to the theory of the demographic transition. Yet, where earlier theorists examined the congruence of fertility and other social changes, the new scholars were interested in the tension between fertility and the established social structure.

New Explanations of Fertility Decline

The recent approaches to the fertility transition have sharply criticized the economic theory of fertility. While granting that economics—the cost of raising children and the opportunity costs to the parents—is important, the new scholars insist that the economic determinants of fertility were tightly constrained by other social structures: the family and culture. Economics made a difference, but only to the extent that the rest of society allowed it.

An Australian demographer, Caldwell based his theory of the fertility decline on his reading of a vast historical and contemporary literature from the West, Africa, and Asia. When the demographic transition theory was first articulated, scholars hoped the West could serve as a model for the experience of the developing world. Ironically, Caldwell used the contemporary experience of the Third World to explore the historical experience of the West.

Caldwell criticizes the economic theory of fertility for its failure to consider the role of social constraints in the fertility transition and its identification of rationality with "utility maximization." He rejects the notion that pretransition societies were somehow less rational. "The fundamental thesis is that fertility behavior in both pretransitional and post-transitional societies is economically rational," he notes, "within the context of socially determined economic goals and within bounds largely set by biological and psychological factors."[29]

Caldwell asserts that in the history of fertility there is a "great divide"—a point where the compass hesitatingly swings around 180°." The logic of the family economy before the divide encourages high fertility, but afterwards favors low fertility. The key to the change is the new flow of resources within the family. Before the divide, the "net flow of wealth is towards parents and . . . hence high fertility is rational," while later the flow is toward the children, which makes lower fertility economically rational.[30]

Caldwell emphasizes that there is no purely economic reason for parents to have children after the swing of the demographic compass. Demographers need not explain why fertility falls, but, rather, why it takes so long: "fertility often falls slowly and even irregularly . . . for social and psychological reasons—the extent to which alternative roles are available to women, the degree to which child-centeredness renders children relatively expensive, the climate of opinion, and so on."[31]

Although a deterministic theory in appearance, Caldwell's concern lies much more with the ideological supports of the family system and the cultural and institutional forces that undermine the older family system. It is this delicate balance of economic and cultural concerns that makes Caldwell's account interesting.

The fertility decline originated in the changing relationship between the family and the economic structure of society. Before the transition, the family is the primary economic unit of society. This "familial mode of production" is anchored in the vertically extended family.

The relative cheapness of raising children and their early entry into productive labor makes them a natural asset. This economic exploitation is supported by social control and socialization. Gerontocracy and the parental control of marriage are direct means of control, while the younger generation is kept in line by a family ideology that stresses the duty of children to their parents, the importance of austere child-rearing, and the priority of family loyalty over universalistic values.

Even after the market economy makes significant inroads into the familial mode of production, its ideology continues to control family life. In Western Europe, for example, the labor market spread selectively. "The familial system in the West depended on a sharp division of labor," Caldwell writes.

> The husband worked outside the home for wages or profits and almost all his input of labor was into these activities, while a wide range of activities (clothing, feeding, providing a clean and comfortable environment, child rearing) was undertaken by the wife with the help of the children (especially the daughters). In effect, then, the husband ran his own highly efficient family-based subsistence system for producing services. Essentially, this was a second (and at least equally important) mode of production in society; the relations of production in the first mode were between employer and employee, but in this second mode they were between a husband and his wife and children.[32]

Thus the family economy was organized in two tiers during the transition from high to low fertility. The traditional family ideology protected the older pattern of exploitation from the market economy. The new economic relations could only affect fertility when the ideological pillars of the older social order were undermined.

The disintegration of the family ideology was largely brought about by the spread of mass education. While education had a number of direct economic impacts on fertility—reducing child labor, increasing the cost of children—its major impacts were ideological: redefining the child as a *future* worker, speeding cultural change, and spreading Western values. Education led to the disintegration of "a family morality, backed by the religion and outlook of the day, that enshrined the value of children living austerely and of children (and wives) working hard and being helpful without making undue complaints or demands."[33]

Yet Caldwell's argument does not apply to the first group to use formal education—the wealthy—who continued to have high fertility after its members sent their children to school. Here, Caldwell resorts to ad hoc arguments. On the one hand, "children did not apparently become a net lifetime economic drain. . . . The rich were so affluent that such losses were of no account." At the same time, education did not have the same ideological impact on the authority of rich parents: "Fathers, too, were educated and in exactly the same system. Educators did not bring the views and morality of another class. Thus, education served as a solvent for working class family morality, but not that of the upper class."[34]

Caldwell has made an immense contribution to the theory of fertility decline. He has called attention to the need to examine the links between macro-level social and economic change and the decisions of individual couples. Furthermore, he has insisted that middle-level institutions—the family, kin groups, and culture—are the crucial mediators. The family economy and ideology together maintained a family system that served, first, as a bulwark against social change and, later, as the conduit for new values. Education decisively changed the economic value of children and their cultural position in the household.

Caldwell has used evidence from around the world over the past three centuries to support his argument. American history, however, presents some problems for his theory.

Caldwell argues that the working class "familial" mode of production was flexible enough to resist full integration into the market economy. Yet, in Michael Katz, Michael Doucet, and Mark Stern's detailed analysis of the family economy of nineteenth-century Hamilton and Buffalo, we found that the family economy was relatively inflexible, unable to adjust

to the consumption needs of the family.[35] Caldwell may have overesti-
mated the continuities between the peasant family and that of the early
industrial working class.

We can question, as well, Caldwell's assertion that working-class
parents retained an exploitative relationship with their children. Caldwell
admits that in the United States the austere view of child rearing had
largely disappeared early in the nineteenth century. While it is true that
North American fertility did begin to decline somewhat by the first decade
of that century, Caldwell's argument does not fully explain why the fertility
rate decline lagged so far behind the disintegration of traditional family
ideology.

This has implications for the role of education in the decline of
fertility. According to Caldwell, education affected fertility primarily by
changing the family ideology. Yet, if high fertility resisted the rise of mass
education, that argument too must be reexamined.

Finally, in his desire to articulate a general theory of fertility, Caldwell too often ignores the impact of social class and ethnicity. These factors
enter his argument only tangentially: the family ideology of workers and
ethnics is slower to break down than that of natives and the well-off. Yet
class and ethnicity did not only affect the beliefs of individuals; they
affected their economic situation and opportunities, as well.

Another group of demographers have used the European Fertility
Project data base to reformulate the theory of the demographic transition.
Like Caldwell, they reject the narrow terms of the economists' argument.
They also share with Caldwell a belief that the decline of fertility lagged
behind the change in children's economic value. Rather than focusing on
the family, however, they view the cultural group as the key to the fertility
transition.

In their important paper of 1979, Knodel and van de Walle identify
four major findings of recent demographic history: fertility declined in a
variety of social, economic, and demographic conditions; the practice of
family limitation was largely absent from pre-transition populations; the
decline in marital fertility was irreversible; and cultural setting influenced
the onset and spread of the fertility decline independently of socioeconomic
conditions.[36]

Knodel and van de Walle's belief that family limitation was alien
to pretransition populations contradicts the findings of other scholars.
Since the publication of Norman Himes's classic work on contraception,

scholars have generally believed that earlier generations used a number of contraceptive techniques. E. A. Wrigley and Gunner Carlsson have argued, in addition, that preindustrial couples responded to economic crises by restricting marital fertility.[37]

Two types of evidence support Knodel and van de Walle's argument: the age structure of fertility and the average age of last birth. Using the "m" statistic developed by Coale and Trussel, Knodel and van de Walle find that "family limitation in Western Europe was either absent or quite minimal (perhaps limited only to special segments of society, such as the social elites) prior to the onset of the long-term decline in marital fertility." Indeed, they believe the "very concept of family limitation was alien to the mentalities of much of the population in the pre-transition era."[38]

Knodel and van de Walle do not deny that marital fertility declined during preindustrial economic crises, but they distinguish this decline— the result of prolonged child spacing—from true family limitation. Child spacing produces a unique age-specific fertility pattern—low rates across the life cycle—while family limitation produces a high, early peak in fertility and then a rapid decline in later years. Knodel and van de Walle argue that family limitation, not child spacing, was central to the European fertility transition.

Yet Knodel and van de Walle's argument raises some tricky historical questions. While twentieth-century theorists may see a clear distinction between "traditional" adjustment methods and the "modern" innovation of family limitation, did nineteenth-century couples draw such a clear line? The European Fertility Project's aggregate data make it impossible for Knodel and van de Walle to pursue this question.

Knodel and van de Walle's theory contradicts Caldwell's on one point: the "rationality" of high fertility among pretransition populations. They believe that "unwanted" births were quite common, but that ignorance of contraception prevented couples from doing anything about their situation. Caldwell, on the other hand, is quite insistent that researchers have misinterpreted their own ignorance as a lack of rationality: "This lack of fertility control within marriage has often been taken to be a sign of ignorance of contraception or of easy acceptance of the inevitable. There is little to support this view."[39]

The lack of nominal data containing information on individual families also prevents Knodel and van de Walle from examining the role of the family. Yet they do insist that the cultural group played an important independent role in promoting fertility decline. They found long-standing patterns of regional fertility variations in nineteenth-century Europe that paralleled those of other cultural differences, including the status of women, language, and political attitudes.

Lesthaeghe also focuses on the role of culture in qualifying the economic theory of fertility. For him, two forces govern the decline: a cost/benefit rationality of individual couples and the imperatives of the social system to maintain a demographic "homeostatic" balance. Like Caldwell, Lesthaeghe argues that as a result of social change, the small family became economically rational before the transition. Lesthaeghe believes the reason for the lag was the coercive role of culture: "long-term demographic homeostasis is the result of enforced, rather than self-imposed restraint."[40]

For Lesthaeghe, when economic development is controlled, the chief variation in fertility is the result of the effectiveness of the old moral order in marshalling its social control. The Church and "the lagging ethical approval" of other cultural institutions enforced society's interest in higher fertility on individual couples. Their power, however, was eventually broken by cultural diversification.

As new subcultures—dissenting religious orders, new political movements, ethnic nationalisms—developed in nineteenth-century Europe, the control of the older order declined. Regional variations in fertility were closely tied to these trends in cultural diversification: "over and beyond the effects of changes in the mode of production and its ramifications with respect to the terms of household economic calculations, diversifications emerged in the timing and format of the marital fertility decline that were closely associated with the development of differential and sometimes compartmentalized ideological codes."[41]

Lesthaeghe's analysis, like Caldwell's, clarifies the limits of the economics of fertility. Once the "compass swing" of household economics occurs, the social system retards the decline of fertility. Rather than entering through the back door of individual tastes, as the economists would have it, social control was a direct force in retarding the decline in fertility. Only a revolution in thought could reduce marital fertility.

Yet Lesthaeghe fails to distinguish between social control—the direct regulation of behavior through law and coercion—from socialization—the indirect regulation of values through training and education. In the United States, where cultural diversity was the norm, the control and sanctions of "society" were difficult to identify. Cultural values and socialization affected the timing of the decline more than direct social coersion.[42]

The source of this fuzziness is the lack of a fully developed theory of culture in the demographic literature. Too often culture is simply equated with ethnicity or region and treated as a black box. If Lesthaeghe, Caldwell, Knodel and van de Walle are right, if culture and ideology are so important to the decline in fertility, then demographers and demographic historians will need to take the concept of culture seriously and integrate anthropological literature into their work.

Conclusion

Recent contributions to European demographic history provide an opportunity to improve our interpretation of North American history. While the differences between America and Europe cannot be ignored, the complex forces that Caldwell and the others have identified can be reformulated to fit the American case. Given the descriptive character of much of the North American literature and its theoretical weaknesses— its reliance on theories of modernization and land availability—a reinterpretation is long overdue.

The chapters that follow interpret the history of fertility in Erie County, New York in light of the contributions of Caldwell, Lesthaeghe, and Knodel and van de Walle. At the same time, they will examine some weaknesses of the theories in the North American context.

First, we will examine the shifts in Erie County's economic and social structure. Two questions are particularly important here: what were the changes in the opportunity structure of the region and how did the family economy respond to these changes?

Next we will examine the social and ethnic differentials in fertility as they developed between 1855 and 1915. What was the timing of the fertility transition and to what extent did different social groups participate in it? We know that not all groups went through the fertility transition at the same time. Our knowledge of why this was so, however, is limited. Did some groups' lag originate in their cultural insularity, or was it tied to their social structure, particularly their economic situation and opportunities?

We are especially interested in the relationship of family strategy and family morality to the rapid decline of poverty in early-twentieth-century Buffalo. The decline of poverty affected working-class families both materially and ideologically. First, it meant that the family had more resources; it could now meet its basic needs. Second, the decline in poverty increased the family's interest in overall planning. Since there were sufficient resources, parents now could decide how they wanted to use them in the future. As the horizon of control lengthened, couples wanted to plan their fertility.

Knodel and van de Walle have made a strong case that pretransition populations knew nothing of contraception, and that family limitation was innovative behavior. We will use the age-specific fertility data from Erie County to examine the extent to which they are right. Did the families of Erie County display a distinctively new pattern of family limitation at the same time that fertility began to decline, or were other patterns present?

The European scholars are increasingly interested in culture's influence on fertility. Whereas culture in Europe is defined regionally, in the United States we will examine ethnicity in conjunction with immigration. Three questions will occupy us:

First, how did culture interact with social structure? Was one more important than the other? Did they act independently of one another, or did one influence the other?

Second, how did the process of cultural change—assimilation—influence fertility? Did intermarriage affect fertility? Did immigrants have higher fertility than their children? Finally, was migration history related to fertility?

Third, what cultural processes affected the timing of the fertility decline? If the economists' model of human action were correct, we would expect fertility to be a product of utility maximization. As the economy changed, families would adjust their fertility for optimal utility. Yet, for the families of Erie County, a different standard—family viability—was more relevant. As long as the old patterns of family life were viable, they did not change. It was only when this criterion was not met that families moved rapidly to find a new pattern.

Taken together, these questions demonstrate the need for a dynamic conceptualization of culture. Neither evolution nor diffusion—the common theories in the social change literature—are capable of explaining historical experience. Social change, at least in this case, is not the story of the slow transition from one set of values and behaviors to another. It was, rather, a sharp break. In a matter of a few years, the families of Erie County abandoned one pattern of social behavior and adopted another.

Education was a key element in the process of social change in Erie County. While most students of fertility recognize its importance, they disagree about why it is so. Caldwell believes that education served to break the exploitative hold of parents on their children. If he were correct, we would expect a lag between the increase in education and the decline in fertility. If the two happened at the same time, another explanation is called for.

Finally, we will examine that venerable issue in American demographic history: rural fertility. As we have seen, rural fertility has generated its own questions and interpretations. Here, we will ask if the same analytical categories that influence urban fertility—social class and ethnicity—can be extended to the countryside.

The history of fertility is a forbidding field. It has its own techniques and methods of analysis, and its own—sometimes arcane—theories. Yet, it is a subject of great relevance to North American social history. The decision to have children, their number and timing, provides us with one of the few glimpses into the private domain of the family. A careful examination of the process of fertility decline allows us to understand better how social and cultural change happen and what their effects are on individuals and families.

2

Economic and Social Development of Buffalo, 1850–1920

BETWEEN the Civil War and World War I, Buffalo changed from a commercial to an industrial city. At midcentury, it had been a modest location for the transfer of raw goods from the West to the markets of the East. Later, the city became a major industrial center as businessmen took advantage of its location for producing finished goods. On the eve of the Great War, Buffalo reached its peak of importance in the national economy, as the eighth largest manufacturing city in the nation and—in the eyes of its boosters—destined to surpass all industrial cities save Chicago and Pittsburgh.

This chapter investigates the emergence of the industrial city and its impact on the city's social life. We focus particularly on three factors: the impact of industrial concentration on the opportunity structure, the segmentation of the Buffalo labor market, and the ethnic stratification of the work force.[1]

Although we are interested in the industrial growth of Buffalo, it was the Erie Canal that dominated the city's economy throughout the period. Buffalo, located at the Canal's western terminus, was one of the nation's most important points for the transshipment of goods. As raw materials were transferred from Great Lakes ships to canal boats or the railroad, it made sense to process them in the city. Thus, the size of Buffalo's manufacturing base reflected the flow of goods along its trade routes.

The Canal and Lakes trade determined, as well, the type of industries in the city. Lumber, wheat, and cattle passed through Buffalo, and as a result, milling, brewing and malting, lumber, and leather dominated the city's manufacturing in 1850. During the last half of the nineteenth century, slaughtering, soap, and furniture became important industries. Finally, the development of the Pennsylvania anthracite coalfields and the Mesabi iron range at the turn of the century turned Buffalo into a steel and chemical center.

In 1860, of the ten leading industries in the nation, as measured by value added, Buffalo was substantially represented in eight of them (Table 2.1). With the exception of footwear and men's clothing, the other leading industries were all heavy manufacture: lumber, flour and meal, iron, machinery, carriage and wagons, and leather. Despite its representation, Buffalo's productivity in these industries was lackluster. Of the

Table 2.1. Value Added and Value Added Per Worker, Buffalo and the United States, 1860, 1900

	United States		Buffalo	
	Value Added	Value Added per	Value	Value Added per
Industry	(millions)	Worker	Added	Worker
1860				
Cotton goods	$ 55	$ 480	—	—
Lumber	54	710	$174,500	$ 590
Boots and shoes	49	400	136,500	340
Flour and meal	40	430	215,600	1,620
Men's clothing	37	320	165,200	340
Iron	36	720	376,900	420
Machinery	33	810	288,200	770
Woolen goods	25	410	—	—
Carriages and wagons	24	650	192,400	920
Leather	23	1,000	753,200	1,780
1900				
Machinery	690	1,290	—	—
Lumber	650	930	2,920,000	970
Printing	540	2,080	5,440,000	1,370
Iron and steel	330	1,370	995,379	1,143
Malt liquor	280	5,010	5,020,000	6,060
Men's clothing	270	1,180	2,350,000	1,040
Cotton goods	260	680	—	—
Tobacco	240	1,440	—	—
Railroad cars	210	730	2,250,000	648
Boot and shoes	180	910	521,000	736

SOURCE: Calculated from U.S. Censuses of Manufactures.

eight, in only three was Buffalo above average in productivity (measured by value added per worker): lumber, flour, and carriage and wagons.

By 1900, Buffalo was represented in seven of the nation's ten leading industries: lumber, printing and publishing, malt liquor, men's clothing, railroad cars, footwear, and iron and steel. Of these seven, however, Buffalo was more productive than average in only two—lumber and malt liquor.

The pace of Buffalo's industrialization was spectacular (Table 2.2). Value added in manufacture—the difference between the value of raw materials and product—grew steadily and impressively. Between 1860 and 1900, the value added by Buffalo's industries increased from $4.8 million to $48.9 million, an average growth rate of six percent per year. Expressed in constant dollars, the growth was even greater, from $4.1 to $58.0 million.[2]

The capital base of the city grew at an annual rate of 7.5 percent. But unlike value added, which slowed down significantly during the depressions of the 1870s and 1890s, growth of capital investment was sustained over the entire period. Capital investment per firm increased from 8,700 dollars in 1860 to 141,600 dollars in 1914.

As the capital of the city grew, so too did its labor force. In 1860 ony 6,500 "hands" labored in the city's manufacturing sector, an average of 8.2 per firm. By the turn of the century, the average was 12.2. During the industrial boom at the beginning of the twentieth century, the figure grew more quickly, reaching 38 workers per establishment in 1909.

These figures do not accurately portray the real concentration of workers, since they average out a few huge firms and many smaller ones. In 1914, the only year for which we have figures broken down by size of firm, the average establishment labor's force was 27.3. Yet only 24 percent of the work force labored in establishments with under fifty workers. Almost an equal number—26 percent—worked in establishments with over 500 workers. The average wage earner was employed in an establishment with 189 workers.

While the average number of workers rose steadily, the average wage did not. In 1860, workers averaged 280 dollars (352 constant dollars) per year. The increase in money wages during the Civil War, however, was cancelled out by inflation. Real wages fell to $298 per year by 1870. During the seventies, the wages of employed workers increased 3.5 percent a year. Wages rose more than a quarter between 1900 and 1914, from 587 to 745 constant dollars.

Table 2.2. Economic Indicators, Buffalo, 1860–1914

Economic Indicator	Census Year						
	1860	1870	1880	1890	1900	1909	1914
Number of establishments	792	1,429	1,183	3,565	3,902	1,964	2,454
Value added[a]	4.8	12.2	15.4	45.9	48.9	99.4	106.8
Capital investment[a]	5.5	13.0	26.8	70.2	103.9	280.1	347.6
Capital per establishment[b]	8.7	7.3	23.2	21.7	31.6	156.1	141.6
Labor force	6,500	13,274	18,021	51,433	47,606	75,085	81,986
Average wage/year	352	298	421	489	587	690	745
Capital per worker	1,070	787	1,523	1,502	2,590	4,085	4,239
Total product[a]	13.6	22.0	43.9	109.3	145.0	306.5	299.0
Labor share of value added[c]	.379	.406	.484	.555	.483	.477	.573

SOURCE: Calculated from U.S. Censuses of Manufacture.
NOTE: All dollar figures are given in constant 1914 dollars.
[a]Figures for value added, capital investment, and total product are in millions of dollars.
[b]Thousands of dollars.
[c]See text for explanation.

Buffalo's wage increase during the depression of the 1870s was not shared with the nation. The real wages of non-farm employees in the United States rose one-half of one percent per year during that decade, one-seventh the increase in Buffalo. The data support William Thurstone's observation in 1874: "Considering the complete derangement of the financial machinery of the United States and the great panic which prevailed in September last, probably no city in the Union suffered less than Buffalo."[2]

Yet this increase in wages was a mixed blessing. It caused a permanent shift in the relative wages of Buffalo in the national economy. During the 1860s and 1870s, Buffalo's wage rates were below the national average by as much as 75 dollars per year. After 1880, they were constantly above average. Buffalo had neither the economic advantage of high productivity nor cheap labor.[4]

The one piece missing from our portrait of Buffalo's industrial economy is perhaps the most important: profitability. Since there is no direct measure of this, we have been forced to rely on a proxy: labor's share of value added (LSVA).[5]

LSVA rose fairly consistently over the period, suggesting a steady decline in profitability. In 1860, labor costs constituted less than 38 percent of value added; by 1890, the figure had risen to 55.5 percent. While the LSVA dropped between 1890 and 1909, it reached 57.3 by 1914. Breaking down these data by industry demonstrates that this rise was not the result of the changing composition of the economy; all industries for which we have data had a rising LSVA over the period.

The experience of Erie County, then, supports Steindl's contention that American business capital growth declined steadily as the economy matured. He writes:

In terms of capital accumulation the decade of the great depression stands out from all the preceding ones as historically unique . . . [Yet, stagnation] did not come overnight. Preceding it there was a long process of secular change, which passed almost unnoticed because memories are short and comparisons over long periods are difficult to make. Hardly anybody during the "New Era" [of the 1920s] was aware of the fact that the annual rate of growth of business capital was only half what it had been thirty years earlier![6]

Few businessmen in Buffalo perceived the decline of profits. In fact, the decline was greater in the city than in the nation as a whole. In 1899,

Buffalo's LSVA was 48.3 and the nation's was 44.3. By 1914, the national figure had declined slightly to 42 percent, but Buffalo's rose to 57 percent.

We have found, then, that neither labor costs, productivity, nor profitability explains Buffalo's economic growth. Although the city's economy continued to expand, it did so because of its past advantages—location and existing infrastructure. As these benefits declined, so too did Buffalo's success.

While the city's economic base broadened between 1860 and 1900, the early twentieth century marked a significant departure. It was then that the city took advantage of the technological innovations of the "second industrial revolution" to transform its industrial base. The three major scientific breakthroughs of this period—in steel, dyes, and motive power—each had an impact on the city's economic order.[7]

Steel and dyes led the transformation. While the metals industry flourished during the 1880s and 1890s, the watershed was the construction of the Lackawanna Steel Company's giant mill just south of Buffalo in 1901–1902. At the same time, the use of coal-tar revolutionized the dye industry.

Coal-tar or aniline dyes had an uneven development in the United States. The industry was retarded by German patents. While this prevented larger concerns from entering the field, smaller producers—like Joseph Schoelkopf—flourished. Schoelkopf, whose father had been a prominent tanner in the city at mid-century, turned Buffalo for a time into the "aniline dye capital" of the United States.

This success was short-lived. During World I, the German patents were revoked, and DuPont Chemical acquired over three hundred of them. Schoelkopf's factory became the cornerstone for the National Aniline and Chemical Company in 1917, but it could not compete with DuPont. Still, dyes remained important to the city's economy through the 1920s.[8]

Buffalo became a leader in electricity generation in 1896 when the hydroelectric potential of Niagara Falls was harnessed, giving the city the cheapest electricity in the nation for a number of years. The cheap energy attracted a variety of industries: brass, tin, copper, steamfitting, and structural iron.

The combination of cheap energy, shipping facilities, and the metal industry attracted automobile makers. In the 1890s, a number of firms began to produce cars, the most important of which was the George Pierce Company, maker of the fabled Pierce Arrow. The Thomas Flyer Motor

Car Company and Ford also produced automobiles in the city in the early twentieth century.

Labor force changes reflected the industrial growth of the period. After 1880, the leading industrial employers were the foundries, which employed 2,200 in 1880 and 4,254 in 1914. The car and general shops of the city were second in employment in both years. A number of capital-intensive industries—brewing, leather, and malting—provided little employment, while two large employers—men's clothing and furniture—were small in capital or value added (Table 2.3).[9]

The Buffalo economy, dominated by heavy industry, provided little paid employment for women. In 1860, 94 percent of the labor force was male, while in 1914, it was 86 percent. By contrast, in 1870 when Buffalo's work force was 92 percent male, only 81 percent of workers in New York State were men. Thirty years later, in 1900, the male share of the labor force in Buffalo was 85 percent, but only 73 percent in the state.

As a result, the leading employers of women were not among the major industries of the city. Women worked in the clothing industry throughout the period. During the early twentieth century, the only additional women's work was in the paper box industry, which became a

Table 2.3. Total Wage-Earners, Leading Industries, Buffalo, 1860–1914

	Census Year				
Industry	1860	1880	1890	1900	1914
Men's clothing	486	1,548	3,222	3,048	1,726
Flour milling	133	201	160	195	749
Leather	422	542	596	561	554
Malt liquor	137	390	523	560	958
Lumber	294	643	2,039	1,573	1,074
Foundry	—	2,200	4,381	3,694	4,254
Malting	—	279	532	205	283
Slaughtering	—	289	766	928	1,557
Soap	—	205	411	743	1,465
Furniture	—	485	1,139	1,243	1,843
Shipbuilding	—	809	538	162	315
Printing	—	612	1,422	1,820	2,027
Car and general shop	—	—	3,343	3,686	3,418
Brass	—	—	—	373	688
Copper and tin	—	—	—	470	533
Paper boxes	—	—	—	374	1,168

SOURCE: Calculated from U.S. Censuses of Manufactures.

notorious employer of immigrant girls. Between 1890 and 1914, the number of women box makers increased from 163 to 700.

The economic statistics of Buffalo hide as much as they illuminate. The wage earners of the manufacturing census were not faceless, nameless workers, but flesh-and-blood people. While their status as wage earners united them, social and cultural forces divided them. The labor force was segmented into a stable and a casual sector, while immigration increased its ethnic diversity.

The Business Class and the City

The business class of Buffalo was caught in an uneasy position throughout the late nineteenth and early twentieth centuries. On the one hand, its members were the beneficiaries of the economic boom; on the other hand, they were concerned that the by-products of the boom—the changing geography, population, and power structure of the city—would undercut this power. Torn by this conflict, Buffalo's businessmen threw themselves intensely into "doing good."

As Robert Kilduff has noted, the development of philanthropy in Buffalo was marked by irony. Buffalo was a well-off city. Its public health, housing, and poverty problems were minor compared to those of New York, Chicago, and Philadelphia. Yet Buffalo was always leading the nation into battle against these problems. Whether developing an urban park system by Frederick Law Olmstead or founding the nation's first Charity Organization Society, Buffalo took up the newest solution to the problems of the emerging industrial order.[10]

The solution to this paradox may lie in the structure of the working class. While some of the working people of Buffalo did suffer from the ills of the early industrial city, this was only a fraction of the population. Unlike the bourgeoisie of London, which feared it would be engulfed by a sea of the "demoralized" or "degenerate," Buffalo's business class saw a set of specific problems that it could solve. The very limits of Buffalo's urban problems may have allowed the business community to take a more positive and active role in their solution.[11]

Optimism swept members of the Buffalo business class in the early twentieth century. They supported commission government and Americanization to assimilate the immigrant and limit his political power, and they supported vocational training to uplift the working population. The business journal of the city crowed:

Although accompanied by great waste, the powerful minority is making a greater effort to put the worker majority on a higher plane of living
than at any time known. The hindrance in the way of speedier consum-
mation of results aimed at comes from the uneducated majority. . . . Taking into account the almost overwhelming task of lifting thousands of
uneducated people and their children up to a fit standard of living, the
public school has justified its right to our admiration and respect.[12]

The elite of Buffalo conformed, then, in many ways to the image of
the Progressive urban elite proposed by Samuel P. Hays. It combined an
interest in Americanization with a distrust of the political power and
independence of the immigrants. It turned to municipal reform to establish
an urban order less susceptible to their power and more responsive to
that of the business community.[13]

The same ambivalence was evident in the business class view of
Buffalo's place in the national economy. The business community was a
cranky and overbearing lot if we are to believe the business press. Like
men a little unsure of their position, they lauded the Queen City a bit
more loudly than might have been justified and were ever-sensitive to
slights and injuries. Their own early sense of manifest destiny was clear
in the 1855 Chamber of Commerce observation:

All the natural advantages makes this city one of the most important
commercial points in the United States. . . . As the West becomes more
largely populated, the demand for manufactured articles increases, and as
our locality obliges us to receive from the West the great bulk of her produce, so it enables us to send forth to her with greatest facility and at the
least expense those articles which she requires in return.[14]

This confidence endured. A half century later, the inevitability of
the city's growth was still a topic of comment: "The vast steel and allied
industries centering at Pittsburgh will of their own volition move within
the boundaries of the State of New York and locate on the Niagara
Frontier. The ore will meet the coke at Buffalo. The manufacturing product will be floated down the Erie Canal instead of being hauled across
the Alleghenies. This is inevitable."[15]

Yet we can challenge these convictions. Buffalo was in constant
competition with the other Lakes cities, especially Cleveland and Detroit;
the Chamber of Commerce journal, the *Live Wire*, continually denounced
Buffalo's competitors. In January 1912, for example, the journal noted:
"Evidently the red rage of jealousy has overtaken the city up the lake
[Cleveland] because of Buffalo's unparalleled business boom and the

unconquerable spirit of progress that possesses her loyal business community." This stance could degenerate into journalistic infantilism, as in 1911, when the *Live Wire* featured a series of songs ridiculing Cleveland, Detroit, and Chicago.[16]

This bravado, however, quickly dissolved when the economy turned sour. In a matter of a few months, the "unconquerable" spirit of the business community was transformed into fears for the city's very existence. As the mood changed, business people looked for scapegoats.

While businessmen often complained about the lack of banking facilities, the lack of internal improvements and the discrimination by the railroads were even more rankling. As early as 1870, William Thurstone of the Chamber of Commerce compared the city's unfavorable railroad rates with those of Detroit and Erie, Pennsylvania.[17]

This soon became the conventional wisdom of the business community. In 1914, for example, the city's lumber exchange brought a suit against over ninety railroads, claiming that they had conspired to discriminate against Buffalo in rate-setting.[18]

Business leaders also worried about the quality of the harbor and the Erie Canal. The Chamber of Commerce called for commitments by the state and federal governments for harbor improvements, while Mayor J. N. Adams pleaded that the city be "emancipated" through improvement of "a port throbbing with commerce and trade, an outer harbor developed and busy and . . . an inner harbor freed from needless obstructions."[19]

Community leaders in the late nineteenth century also lobbied the state legislature to stop the decline of the Canal. In response, the legislature suspended tolls on the Canal during the 1880s and authorized construction of the vast New York State Barge Canal system at the turn of the century. Yet, despite a temporary rise in traffic, these improvements could not counterbalance the declining advantage of the city's location.[20]

The outlook of the business community of Buffalo was filled with contradictions. It could look forward to Buffalo's becoming the second city of the United States, while worrying that the grain and lumber trades were about to collapse. It cheered the constructive role of the Polish Businessmen's Association in the fight for vocational education, while fearing the increased political clout of the immigrant vote. It was filled with expectations of future wealth and with fears of the decline of old wealth, anxious for the rise of enlightened consciousness and uneasy about the threats posed by immigrants, railroads, and the state legislature.

These contradictions were, in part, a response to the changing fortunes of the business class. The same forces that changed the economic and physical landscape also altered social relations. The occupational and ethnic composition of the city was shaken, and the class experiences of the business and working classes were permanently changed.

Economic Development and Social Structure

Buffalo's economic growth transformed its class and ethnic structure. The rise of the corporation increased the number of managers and business employees and reorganized the labor market for manual workers. As immigrants and their children became concentrated as specific elements of the labor force, the interaction of social class and ethnicity gave the city a distinctive social structure, segmented into a stable primary sector and a unstable secondary market, as we shall explain shortly.

Buffalo was born an immigrant city. At midcentury, German and Irish immigrants dominated its population. After 1880, Poles, Italians, and Russian Jews became prominent; together, these three composed 16 percent of the city's household heads by 1915.

In 1855, nearly half of the household heads of the city were German, while the American-born and Irish represented 21 and 17 percent, respectively (Table 2.4). The German share had declined to 19 percent by 1900, although another 39 percent of the household heads were of German ancestry. Only four percent of the household heads were Irish-born in 1900 but another ten percent had Irish parents. Thus, while 52 and 62 percent of household heads were native-born in 1900 and 1915, they were not Yankee. Only 21 percent of the household heads, in fact, had American-born fathers in 1900.

The rough outlines of the occupational structure, too, changed markedly. In 1855, over half of those household heads who had a classifiable occupation were skilled workers. This proportion fell to about forty percent in 1900 and 1915, while the number in other manual work occupations (transport, unskilled labor, etc.) remained relatively stable between 1855 and 1900 (28 percent in 1855 and 31 percent in 1900) and then fell sharply to 23 percent in 1915.[21]

The decline in the proportion of household heads in working-class occupations was not offset by a rise in the traditional commercial

Table 2.4. Occupational and Ethnic Distribution, Household Heads, Buffalo, 1855, 1900, 1915

Birthplace	Occupational Stratum	Census Year 1855	Census Year 1900	Census Year 1915
Native-born	(N)	(1,185)	(1,773)	(2,720)
	Old business	36.2	22.8	20.6
	New business	14.2	16.1	21.7
	Skilled workers	36.0	39.6	40.1
	Other workers	13.6	21.6	17.4
Canada	(N)	(208)	(179)	(157)
	Old business	22.4	18.1	19.8
	New business	6.7	19.3	25.8
	Skilled workers	50.8	41.1	37.5
	Other workers	20.2	21.5	16.9
Ireland	(N)	(1,550)	(130)	(79)
	Old business	12.2	20.8	44.5
	New business	1.3	10.0	10.6
	Skilled workers	31.8	32.5	31.4
	Other workers	54.6	36.7	13.5
Germany	(N)	(4,424)	(643)	(346)
	Old business	8.5	12.6	16.0
	New business	0.8	4.2	5.7
	Skilled workers	66.2	54.3	57.9
	Other workers	24.5	28.8	19.8
Poland	(N)	—	(332)	(383)
	Old business	—	4.3	10.8
	New business	—	2.4	3.7
	Skilled workers	—	20.2	43.3
	Other workers	—	73.0	42.2
Italy	(N)	—	(85)	(251)
	Old business	—	11.5	16.8
	New business	—	1.3	5.6
	Skilled workers	—	12.9	24.7
	Other workers	—	74.3	52.7
Russia	(N)	—	(22)	(127)
	Old business	—	22.7	32.2
	New business	—	9.1	6.0
	Skilled workers	—	31.8	33.4
	Other workers	—	36.4	27.9
All groups	(N)	(9,189)	(3,181)	(4,387)
	Old business	16.7	17.9	19.7
	New business	4.0	11.9	16.5
	Skilled workers	51.6	39.7	40.6
	Other workers	27.7	30.5	23.1

Table 2.4.   (*Continued*)

Birthplace	Occupational Stratum	1855	Census Year 1900	1915
Place of Birth				
	Native born	20.5	52.4	60.0
	Canada	2.3	5.3	3.6
	Ireland	16.9	3.8	1.8
	Germany	48.1	19.0	7.9
	Poland	—	9.8	8.7
	Italy	—	2.5	5.7
	Russia	—	0.7	2.9
	Other	13.2	4.5	9.4
	TOTAL	100.0	100.0	100.0

SOURCE: Calculated from Federal and New York State Census manuscripts; Buffalo business directories.
NOTES: N's refer to the weighted number in the study sample. Occupational percentages exclude those in other occupations and the missing cases. Old business occupations include merchants and agents, services and semi-professionals, government employees, masters and manufacturers, and clerks. New business occupations include other business employees and professionals. Skilled occupations include those with specific craft designations, while other workers include any other manual labor titles. Percentages do not always total 100 because of rounding.

occupations—merchants, manufacturers, and clerks—who had dominated the business class in 1855. Rather, it was the new commercial occupations—business employees and professionals—which increased most quickly. In 1855, only four percent of household heads were in the "new business" stratum, but by 1915 one in seven (17 percent) were.

These figures hide important shifts in subcategories. In the old business class, government employees increased from one to five percent of the labor force. At the other end of the occupational hierarchy, the ranks of casual laborers were decimated. In both 1855 and 1900 it was the single largest occupation in the city, composing 16 percent of the labor force. By 1915, its share had fallen to 8 percent.

In mid-nineteenth-century Buffalo, ethnicity and occupation were closely related. While only one in five household heads were in a business-class occupation, among natives, the ratio was one in two. The immigrants, on the other hand, were overwhelmingly workers—86 percent for Irish, 91 percent for Germans.

By the turn of the century, the ethnic stratification of the work force was muddied. Sixty-one percent of natives were then workers, many of them second- or third-generation ethnics. At the same time, many from the earlier immigrant groups had joined the business class. The Irish entered government employment; from 2 percent in 1855, the proportion of Irish in government rose to 21 percent by 1915. The Germans, by contrast, became manufacturers (7 percent).

The newer immigrant groups also changed occupations between 1900 and 1915. The proportion of all Poles who were in the "old" business stratum increased from 4 to 11 percent, while those in skilled occupations rose from 20 to 43 percent. Thus, the 30 percent of Polish household heads who were laborers in 1915 was less than half the proportion in 1900.

The Russians (most of them Jewish) were too small a group for accurate occupational distribution for 1900. Compared to the Italians and Poles in 1915, however, they were quite well off. They were over 50 percent more likely to be in the old business stratum than the population as a whole (32 percent to 20 percent) and had a much smaller share in non-skilled occupations than the other new immigrants.

The immigrants entered the occupational structure of the city at the bottom and used different ladders to climb it. Poles moved into manu-facturing, while many Russian- and Italian-born became peddlers and shopkeepers. Germans, who had dominated the skilled labor market at midcentury, moved into factory ownership, while the Irish used politics to advance.

Still, by 1915, only Irish and Canadians had substantially escaped the working class. Those other immigrants who did enter business occu-pations remained distinct from the Yankee business class. More often than not, they were shopkeepers in their ethnic neighborhood or manufacturers for an immigrant market. Significantly, none of the immigrant groups had even half the representation of the native-born in the new business stratum—business employees and professionals. The leading section of the business class continued to be native-born.

The Division of the Business Class

As industrialization and the concentration of ownership continued, members of the native-born business class were increasingly forced out of "old business" (personal business proprietorship). By 1915, more native-born household heads were in "new business" occupations, as business employees or professionals, rather than proprietors or manufacturers. This occupational change had far-reaching consequences. It split the business class in two. Each stratum had its own social status, family strategy, and world view. The new business stratum, in particular, had to struggle to establish an identity of its own.

The traditional professions—law and medicine—trace their origins back over centuries. Yet, in early nineteenth-century America, their status was tenuous. Only later did they establish a solid economic and social position. As Robert Wiebe notes:

> Early in the nineteenth century, widespread hostility toward privilege in a land of opportunity and pell-mell expansion in a land of weak communication had combined to destroy the traditional standards surrounding most occupations and to isolate those few who still maintained a high degree of skill. . . . As this society crumbled, the specialized needs of an urban industrial system came as a godsend to a middle stratum in the cities. . . . Increasingly, formal entry requirements into their occupations protected their prestige through exclusiveness.[22]

In early and mid-nineteenth century America, professionals passed on their skills through apprentice-like arrangements, for example, reading law in an established office. This method allowed, even encouraged nepotism. Professional skill was a form of property; it not only gave one an edge in the labor force, but could be passed on directly to one's children.

The development of formal entry requirements and professional schools changed that. While nepotism was still possible, formal requirements decreased the inheritability of professional standing. Education and training became the path of professional status attainment.

The defenders of the old system often battled the advocates of the new. In mechanical engineering, for example, Monte Calvert found two distinct cultures: a "shop culture" tied to the old apprentice system and a "school culture" connected to the new professional schools.

Shop culture was a "personal affair." With no formal standards, apprentices were often youths that the master "took to." Not surprisingly, most came from the same class as the masters. This "does not suggest collusion," according to Calvert, as much as "that early mechanical engineers (who constituted a self-recognized elite) found it more pleasant and practical to work closely with those they could trust, converse with intelligently, and—not to be discounted—see socially."[23]

By contrast, the school culture stressed formal standards—credentials and test scores—in judging a man's worth. "Formal education was seen by the educators as the coming instrument of social and economic mobility. By the 1920s, candidates for degrees . . . were coming from the lower middle class and receiving unexpected gains in status from their studies."[24]

At the same time, the work context of professionals changed. Many of the newer professions, like engineering, worked directly for corporations. Even members of the old professions, while independent, found themselves enmeshed in larger organizations—law firms and hospitals—which separated them from the marketplace.

The change in the work situation of business employees paralleled that of the professionals. The clerk, who had been the lieutenant to the captain of industry, found his position undermined by the new division of labor and specialization. In place of the all-knowledgeable clerk, dozens of business occupations—accountants, bookkeepers, shipping clerks—entered the office. As Harry Braverman noted: "While it is probable that some of the clerks [of the nineteenth century] . . . correspond roughly to the modern clerical workers in function and status, it is for various reasons more accurate to see the clerical workers of the present . . . era as virtually a new stratum."[25]

The changing circumstances of professionals and business employees and their increased numbers split the business class. Members of the new business stratum no longer aspired to own business property. Furthermore, with the rise of formal entrance requirements, fathers could no longer pass on their position to their sons; education became the path to social status.

If social class were simply a matter of property, the new and old business strata would have been different classes. But other considerations—life style, political views, and authority structures—united these groups.

Ethnicity played an important role. On the one hand, the common culture and ancestry of the native-born old and new business families served to bridge the economic differences between them; on the other hand, ethnicity divided the native merchant class from the important ethnic business groups.

The remaking of the business class was complex. At the work place, the rise of the distinction between mental and manual labor—one rarely made in the entrepreneurial economy—was reinforced by the cult of efficiency and the transformation of the work ethic described by Daniel

Rodgers. Equally important were changes in the patterns and meaning of consumption.[26]

The Division of the Working Class

At midcentury, the experiences of unskilled and skilled workers were converging. The breakdown of skilled trades and the development of the factory served to reduce the barriers between the two segments of the working class. A single working class was emerging.[27]

As the nineteenth century drew to a close, however, this trend was reversed. The industrial development of Buffalo brought about an important division in its working class. By 1900, the city had two working classes, separated by geography and working conditions.

The primary sector was composed of skilled workers. At midcentury, these workers had labored in the city's small workshops and construction sites; but with industrialization, a real factory-based industrial proletariat emerged. The secondary sector was based on the waterfront and the transport sector of the city. It included the specific transport occupations—teamsters, grain scoopers—and many of the city's casual laborers.

The split in the world of the worker was evident in the structure of unemployment. Although workers of all kinds suffered from chronic unemployment, it was concentrated in the secondary stratum of transport workers and laborers. The most secure occupations were those in the primary sector. These included machinists, butchers, tailors, and shoemakers, for whom the unemployment rate for 1889 was less than eight percent.

The building trades experienced short-term seasonal unemployment, but predictable and steady work during much of the year. For example, 19 percent of Buffalo's carpenters had been unemployed at some point in 1889, but only 8 percent had been out of work for over three months. Painters (21 and 12 percent), masons (40 and 23 percent), and steel workers (12 and 6 percent) had similar work histories.

In the secondary stratum, unemployment was common and long-term. Of the fifteen thousand laborers in the city in 1890, 35 percent had been unemployed during the previous year and 26 percent had been out of work for over three months. Among canalmen, boatmen, pilots, and sailors 56 percent had been idled, during the previous year 53 percent for over three months.[28]

Unionization played an important, but limited, role in structuring some occupations. The strong brewers' union contributed to the 259 percent increase in their real wages between 1860 and 1914, compared with the city's average of 85 percent.

Less skilled occupations, like the grain scoopers, also benefited from organization. According to Sidney Levy, the grain scoopers were tyrannized during the late nineteenth century by a saloon-boss system that controlled work and wages. During the 1890s, the union wrested power from the bosses. After the strike of 1899, annual contracts and a closed-shop requirement regularized employment.[29]

The growth of the primary stratum of the working class and the steady rise of wages improved the material condition of working-class families. Once the devastating depression of the 1890s had passed, at least part of the working class began to live without the constant spectre of poverty.

By 1918, the working class could be divided into three income groups. The lowest—laborers, transport workers, and service occupations—earned incomes below what Oscar Ornati has called the "minimum adequacy" income of $1,330 a year. The second group, factory workers, earned incomes between $1,100 and $1,500, with an average of $1,391. At the top of the hierarchy were construction and other skilled workers with wages in the $1,300 to $1,700 range and an average of $1,501.[30]

The laborers and transport workers who composed the lowest strata of the working class experienced extreme deprivation. Using Ornati's "minimum adequacy" as a poverty line, fully 70 percent of laborers, 67 percent of transport workers, and 71 percent of service employees were living in poverty in 1918. On the other hand, the factory and skilled workers, while not affluent, had achieved a level of income and security unknown to nineteenth-century workers.

The rise in living standards, reinforced by the spread of cheap consumer goods and revolving credit, sharply divided the life-styles of the poor and non-poor. The secondary sector of laborers, transport workers, and service workers spent more than a third of their family income on food—a conventional measure of poverty—while the better-off workers spent less than a third. The poor spent a greater portion of their food budget on potatoes and bread, the mainstays of the nineteenth-century worker, while compared to them the better-off spent sixty percent more on meat.

Clothing, too, was a indicator of the improved condition of the primary workers. By 1920, the Lynds noted:

> Even among the men, including working class men, it is apparently less common today than in the nineties to renounce any effort at appearing well-dressed by speaking scornfully of "dudes." "They're no longer content with plain, substantial, low-priced goods . . . but demand 'nifty' suits that look like those every one else buys and like they see in the movies." Speaking of children's clothing, the same merchant said, "Poor mothers come in today with the attitude that 'My boy is just as good as any other boy,' and they often spend for a suit alone enough to buy a plainer suit, shoes, stockings, and cap."[31]

In fact, the clothier's perception was slightly flawed, at least if Middletown was like Buffalo. The poorest families spent less than others on children's clothing both in dollars and as a proportion of their income. Rather, "nifty" clothes became common among the non-poor factory and skilled-worker families.

The working class split in expenditures on leisure as well. The better-off stratum spent an average of $18 during 1918 on movies, compared to $2 among the poor. At the same time, the proportion of income spent on more traditional leisure items—books and newspapers—was negatively correlated with income.

While the working class was stratified by income and poverty, these divisions were not stable. Families moved in and out of poverty depending upon the availability of work, luck, and other resources on which the family could call.

Poverty had an important impact on the family life-cycle. During the nineteenth century, working-class families experienced a predictable cycle of poverty and affluence tied to the number and ages of their members and their ability to work. Typically, a young couple would be relatively well-off, then descend into poverty with the arrival of its children. As the children entered the work force, the family's economic situation would improve. Then, with all children gone, the old couple would again be impoverished.

To cope with these waves of poverty and relative affluence, the family adopted a variety of strategies. The most effective was child labor, which made a tremendous difference, especially if the children were boys who commanded higher wages than girls. Homeownership could serve as a means of forced savings, especially as a preparation for old age. Owning a home, too, could provide a secondary source of income through lodgers or boarders. Finally, families might call upon a wider kin network to provide gifts, loans, or in some instances to take care of a child during extreme emergencies.

As poverty declined, these strategies were abandoned. No longer harried by deprivation, parents could take a more orderly and longer-term approach to planning their lives. Children no longer had to be pulled out of school to go to work. Homeownership became more common as incomes increased, but the home was for the family, not boarders. Since families had less reason to call on other kin for aid, they also had less incentive to provide assistance to each other. Affluence encouraged the separation of the nuclear family.

These divisions in the material condition of the working class were obvious in the lives of individual families included in the Bureau of Labor Statistics's 1918 cost-of-living survey.

Take, for example, the Mooreheads.[33] Mr. Moorehead, a 46-year-old janitor, earned only $900 during the year, which would have left the family in poverty. But three of his four sons were at work; the 18-year-old was a tinsmith, and the 16- and 15-year-olds were laborers. Together, the three contributed $1,570, sixty percent of the family's income. Thus, in spite of Mr. Moorehead's low earnings, the family ended the year with a surplus of $300.

For the Mooreheads, the old family strategy was working. The husband, although poorly paid, was employed and the children had left school to work. Yet, even in the wartime boom, this strategy was precarious. Any number of vagaries—unemployment, sickness—would send the family into crisis.

Equally important, the Mooreheads had enough workers available. What was their situation five years earlier when the children were too young, and what would it be in a few years when the parents were left alone? Indeed, if the boys had been girls with only domestic service or the box factories to choose from, the situation would have been very different.

The O'Sullivans did not share the Mooreheads' luck. Mr. O'Sullivan, a crane operator, earned $1,404 during the year—more than fifty percent more than Mr. Moorehead. Yet his family was younger; none of his four children was employed. Thus, with a garden and gifts, the family's income was only $1,443.

Faced with a shortfall, the family cut expenditures. While the Mooreheads spent $900 on food, the O'Sullivans spent only $668. In desperation, they sold their house for $1,400, keeping them above water.

Was this family in crisis? Yes and no. True, they were forced to cut back on spending and sell the family home. But, from another perspective, they were responding successfully to a predictable crisis. With no children at work, the parents may have bought the house earlier in their marriage as a hedge against this possibility. In the next few years with luck, a daughter or two might enter the work force and relieve the pressure on family resources.

At the same time that the Mooreheads and O'Sullivans retained an old strategy, others moved to a new one. The Jones family included a 42-year-old brewer, his 32-year-old wife, and a five-year-old son. Mr. Jones's income of $1,352 was sufficient to provide for their needs. Just as important, he was a union member (he spent $24 on dues), which suggests that his work was more stable. This predictability meant that the old hedges—homeownership, child labor—were not necessary. Stability and increased wages were the foundations for a new family strategy.

By 1918, the working-class families of Buffalo were caught between the gray, cold poverty of the nineteenth century and the prosperity of the "New Era" of the 1920s. The image of the poverty-stricken proletarian sending his children off to work, ill-clothed and ill-fed, was no longer accurate. While poverty was still common among laborers and transport workers, the families of the upper stratum lived in heated, if spartan, homes, ate meat regularly, kept their children in school, and went to the movies every week or so. The material changes of the working-class families gave birth to a distinctive family strategy and culture.

Conclusion

Buffalo's social and economic history during the late nineteenth and early twentieth centuries makes it a microcosm of the changes that were sweeping industrial America. Of course, no city can be representative of an entire nation's experience. But Buffalo's ethnic composition, rapid growth, and industrial composition make it representative of the experience of a large number of Northern cities.

Buffalo's rapid industrial growth had three impacts on the strategies and fertility of the city's families: it provided few opportunities for women's work, it altered the structure of the business class, and it divided the working class into poor and non-poor segments.

The availability of women's work had a tremendous impact on the family life of some communities, particularly that of textile towns. Communities like Cohoe, New York, Lowell, Massachusetts, and the textile towns of New Hampshire cannot be understood without considering women's work. Obviously, in Buffalo, where women's work was limited, this was not an important factor.[33]

Yet we should not overstate this problem. Textiles were practically the only nineteenth-century industry to provide factory employment to married women. While wage labor was an important feature of women's lives, most of its growth was among single women. As Louise Tilly and Joan Scott have noted, married women generally continued to work within the home.[34]

The changing industrial order of Buffalo did, however, alter the context of white-collar work. The entrepreneurial class of the commercial city was split into two strata: an old business class of merchants and manufacturers and a new stratum of professionals and business employees. While common ethnicity and culture pulled these groups together, their structural situation and family strategies separated them.

At the same time, the working class too was splintering. While the experience of skilled and unskilled workers had converged at midcentury, by the turn of the twentieth century, a new system of stratification, a stable primary sector and an unstable secondary sector, split the working population. This division was reinforced by ethnicity; the natives and old immigrants were predominantly in the primary sector, while most of the new immigrants were in the secondary sector.

This division affected the material conditions of the two strata. The primary sector of construction, factory, and skilled workers emerged from poverty around the turn of the century, while the secondary stratum of laborers and transport workers remained poor.

The decline of poverty sharply altered the family economy and strategy of the well-off workers. The props of the old structure—child labor, boarding, low consumption—were abandoned and a new family strategy emerged. Children stayed in school longer and the family became more nuclear.

Fertility was a fundamental element of these changes in Buffalo. As families struggled to understand and respond to the new social conditions around them, family limitation became an option. The same situation that discouraged child labor and encouraged extended education also put pressure on parents to limit their family size.

Yet the opportunity structure did not provide an equal chance for all families: natives had a better chance than immigrants, business people a better chance than workers. At the same time, differential subcultures and ethnicity often served to preserve older patterns. Thus, other sets of forces influenced the family strategies of Erie County.

This interweaving of factors produced what appears to be a bewildering pattern of fertility. Some groups' fertility declined quickly; others' remained high. Still, by 1915, most families had much lower fertility than they had had in 1855. Before we can fully understand these patterns, however, we must try to disentangle them.

3

Differential Fertility in Erie County: Occupation and Ethnicity

Bᴇᴛᴡᴇᴇɴ 1850 and 1915, Buffalo experienced both dramatic industrial growth and a decline in fertility. The old tradition of the demographic transition would have pointed to the correlation of these two experiences and explained them both as part of the "modernization" of society.

Yet, the more closely we examine the historical evidence and the theory, the less compelling this explanation is. Caldwell and other recent demographers have examined the weakness of the theory. At the same time, the work of American and European historical demographers over the past decade has thrown into question the simplicity of the connection between modernization and fertility decline.

The next three chapters examine the fertility patterns in Erie County and try to make sense of them. In Chapter Four, we take up the development of education and its relationship to the fertility decline. Then in Chapter Five, we turn to rural fertility and examine the continuities between the fertility experience of the city and the countryside.

In the present chapter, we describe the fertility decline. Then we turn to three sets of analytical issues: the process of fertility decline, its cost/benefit logic, and the role of cultural forces in its timing and magnitude.

Was fertility limitation a break with past family experience or simply a modification of it? Knodel and van de Walle have claimed that family limitation was a major innovation in family practice linked to a shift in *mentalité*. Other scholars, in particular Wrigley and Carlsson, have argued that it was simply the adjustment of traditional limitation strategies to new social circumstances.

Whatever the shortcomings of the economic theory of fertility, it is clear that the structure of the economy and the family's response to it have an important influence on fertility. But does the economy affect all social groups in the same way? Obviously not. We will examine the role of social class and the opportunity structure of industrial society on fertility.

While the economic logic of fertility was important, it was not its sole determinant. As Clifford Geertz has argued, rather than seeing culture and social structure as "fitting" together, social change forces us to examine the independent influence of social structure and the meanings that individuals attach to social reality.[1]

In Erie County, culture was tied closely to ethnicity and migration. The historical experience of the immigrants and their interpretation of that experience had a powerful impact on fertility. For some, the logic of the new economic order overwhelmed the traditional patterns, while for others, the old maintained its strength. The pace of the fertility decline was a consequence of these subtle interactions.

The Data

This study is based on one of the largest sets of data ever assembled to investigate fertility in a single community. In total we have gathered data on over 130,000 individuals and 25,000 families over a period of sixty years.[2]

The important methodological point of this study, however, is that we have gathered data on individual families rather than aggregate data on towns, counties, or states. These data allow us to disentangle the influence of occupation from that of ethnicity, the impact of school attendance from that of migration history. In contrast to most of the major studies in historical demography, we can ask the kinds of questions implied by current theories.

The measure of fertility that we have used in this chapter and those that follow is the *fertility ratio* or the child-woman ratio. This measures the number of children, ages 0–5, per one thousand married women, ages 20–49, in a given group. Thus, a fertility ratio of 1,230 for Germans indicates that in households with German parents, there were on average 1.23 young children per household. Sometimes, we report *age-specific* ratios, that is, the fertility ratio for women in a specific age group.

While this measure has been used widely, a number of factors can make it unreliable: underenumeration, the age-structure of the population, and mortality, in particular. All of the figures reported in this study have been age standardized and many have been corrected for mortality.[3]

The Decline of Fertility

Between 1855 and 1915, marital fertility in Erie County fell dramatically. In 1855, for every one thousand women between the ages of 20 and 49, there were 1,235 young children (corrected for mortality). By 1900, the figure for the city of Buffalo had fallen to 1,026, a decline of 17 percent or 0.53 percent a year. During the first 15 years of the new century, fertility fell even more rapidly, declining to 819 per thousand in 1915.

All groups did not reduce their fertility at the same rate. Rather, sharp and persistent differentials were present in fertility. The most important of these differentials were among occupational categories and among ethnic groups.

Social Class and Occupation

Buffalo's economy was transformed during the late nineteenth and early twentieth centuries. Occupation and place in the economy had a huge impact on one's economic condition and opportunities. How were these differences related to fertility?

To answer this question, we need a system of occupational classification that is sensitive to the fissures in the social structure and their change over time. This is no easy task. First, we need to reduce a fluid set of social relations to a static set of categories. Second, for purposes of comparisons we need a classification system that will work as well for the social structure of the mid-nineteenth-century commercial city as for the early twentieth-century industrial metropolis.

Social class is difficult to operationalize. Indeed, attempts to do so have generated their own field in sociology and social history. The problem is implicit in the concept. Class refers to a set of social relations and the process through which these relations are structured over time. People are not "members" of a class; they define "class" as they live their lives.

The result of this process—social stratification—is easy to measure, but is a different order of phenomenon. As Giddens noted:

> The distinction between class and stratum is again a matter of signifi-
> cance, and bears directly upon the problem of class "boundaries." For
> the division between strata, for analytical purposes, may be drawn very
> precisely, since they may be set upon a measurement scale—as, for
> example, with "income strata." The divisions between classes are never
> of this sort; nor, moreover, do they lend themselves to easy visualization,
> in terms of any ordinal scale of "higher" and "lower," as strata do.[4]

In *The Social Organization of Early Industrial Capitalism,* Michael Katz, Michael Doucet, and I argued that the class structure of mid-nineteenth century Hamilton, Ontario, and Buffalo, New York, could best be understood as dominated by two classes, which we called the business class and working class. As we wrote:

> It has taken a corps of research assistants, the most modern electronic
> data-processing equipment, and powerful statistical techniques to make a
> case for what most late nineteenth-century social commentators would
> have accepted without argument. They knew that a great change in
> social organization had taken place and that two great classes, Capital
> and Labor, were increasingly dominating social, economic, and political
> life.[5]

Our investigation of the social history of Buffalo suggests, however, that this class structure was not stable between 1855 and 1915. The pressures which had united each of these two classes were replaced by centrifugal forces which split them apart. The business class was divided between those who continued to own business property—shops or factories—and those who did not. At the same time, the working class was transformed by labor market segmentation. Those workers in the primary sector had more stable work and were less poor than the secondary sector. Thus, the two-class model does not fit the early-twentieth-century city.

To capture these profound shifts in the class structure, we are forced to rely upon the data that the census collected on occupation. These data are supplemented here, as in our earlier study, by data on business ownership that allowed us to differentiate masters and manufacturers from wage workers in the skilled crafts.[6]

As in *The Social Organization of Early Industrial Capitalism*, we have used a ten-category occupational classification to capture these shifts over time: six business groups and four worker groups.

The two major groups among the old business class are the merchants and the manufacturers who controlled the city's commerce and production. In addition, we distinguish other commercial occupations—dealers and semi-professionals—and the government employees. Taken together, these four groups compose the old business class.

The group that grew most quickly over the period of this study was the non-propertied business occupations. The professionals included not only those in traditional professions like medicine and law, but also newer ones, like engineering and architecture. On the other hand, business employees included a wide range of occupations that managed the large industrial enterprises or labored in the office and salesroom.[7] These two groups together make up the new business class.

The major categories in the working class were the skilled workers and the laborers. In addition, we distinguish transport workers (teamsters, draymen, etc., who were crucial to the port) from an "other working class" group, which includes peddlers, waiters, and a variety of manual occupations that did not fit into the other groups.[8]

We occasionally collapse these worker categories to capture the split between the primary and secondary labor markets. To do so, we have differentiated the skilled workers from the other, "non-skilled" workers.

In 1855, high fertility was common among most occupational groups in the city (Table 3.1). Only professionals and business employees had fertility ratios below 1,200 per thousand. While the professionals, with a ratio of 954 per thousand, had a fertility ratio that was well below the average, the other groups' ratios ranged from the business employees' 1,190 per thousand to 1,374 per thousand among "other workers."[9]

The difference between the business and working class was much clearer in 1900. While the professionals continued to have the lowest fertility (637 per thousand), several other business class groups were close behind: government employees (645 per thousand), masters and manufacturers (662 per thousand), dealers and semi-professionals (667 per thousand), and business employees (673 per thousand). Only the merchants' and agents' fertility remained high among those in the business class.

Working class families, by contrast, remained large. All worker groups had higher fertility than the most fertile business class group. Still, for

Table 3.1. Standardized Fertility Ratio, by Occupational Categories, Corrected for Mortality, Buffalo, 1855, 1900, 1915

Occupational Category			Census Year			
	(N)	1855	(N)	1900	(N)	1915
Merchants, agents	(511)	1,213	(217)	758	(343)	663
Manufacturers, masters	(361)	1,314	(131)	662	(222)	790
Service/semi-professional	(103)	1,253	(130)	667	(164)	563
Government employees	(65)	1,343	(141)	645	(257)	675
Professionals	(202)	954	(89)	637	(138)	542
Business employees	(226)	1,190	(313)	673	(685)	550
Skilled workers	(3609)	1,308	(1331)	973	(2068)	792
Transport workers	(326)	1,231	(228)	988	(406)	874
Other workers	(161)	1,374	(153)	1,083	(318)	986
Laborers	(1,458)	1,331	(710)	1,465	(423)	1,347

SOURCE: Calculated from U.S. Census manuscripts, 1900, and New York State Census manuscripts 1855, 1915.

three of the four groups, fertility had fallen between twenty and thirty percent. The laborers of the city—still the largest single occupation—were the big exception. Not only was their fertility higher than that of other workers, it was higher than it had been in 1855.

Three levels of fertility were common, then, among occupational groups. The business class had the lowest fertility—in the 600 per thousand range—while the working class was considerably higher, but divided between the lower rates of the skilled and transport workers and the higher fertility of laborers and other workers.

These data represent current fertility, the number of children born in the previous five years. In 1900, we also have a *cumulative* measure of fertility—children-ever-born—which allows us to examine how recent were the current fertility patterns.

The children-ever-born data pose a methodological problem. The only true measures of completed fertility are for women over 45 years of age. Yet most of these older women had completed their child bearing during the 1880s or before, and so their effect on the current fertility rate was negligible. Furthermore, we do not want to underplay the fertility data for younger women. In order to address this problem, we have used complex multiple regression statistics to estimate completed fertility using data on women of all ages.[10]

The data on children-ever-born generally confirm the differentials we found in the fertility ratios (Table 3.2). The "new" business class—professionals and business employees—had a completed fertility of 3.5 children in 1900, compared to the 4.1 children of the "old" business class. The skilled workers' completed fertility was less than 5.2 children, while that of non-skilled workers was more than 5.7 children. In percentage terms, the cumulative differences within the business class were larger than those for current fertility; among workers, the differences were smaller.

What do these data tell us about the recency of the fertility decline? Completed fertility is based on women who had their children during the past several decades. If differences in children-ever-born are less than those in the current fertility data, we can conclude that the differential has increased recently. By contrast, if differentials in children-ever-born data are larger than those in current fertility, we could speculate that the differential has been reduced in recent years.

Using this logic, the 1900 occupational data suggest that the differential in the business class was by then declining. The new business class's fertility had declined earlier than that of the old business class, but by the end of the century, the traditional business groups were catching up.

In contrast, the working-class differentials appear to be new. Among older women, there was relatively little difference between skilled and non-skilled workers, but in the current fertility data, the differences were pronounced.

Table 3.2. Estimated Children-Ever-Born at Age 50, by Occupation, Erie County, 1900

Occupational Stratum	(N)	Number of Children Ever Born
Old business	(758)	4.15
New business	(479)	3.54
Skilled workers	(1,517)	5.18
Non-skilled workers	(1,322)	5.74
Agricultural workers		
Proprietors	(307)	4.21
Non-proprietors	(145)	3.87

SOURCE: Calculated from U.S. Census manuscripts.
NOTE: These data are derived from a multiple-regression of children-ever-born by the natural logarithm of age for each group. The age of 50 was then placed in the resulting equation to estimate total fertility by that age.

Fertility then fell dramatically among almost all occupational groups between 1900 and 1915. Four of the six business groups recorded declines ranging from the 123 per thousand decline among business employees to the more modest reductions among those in service and semi-professional, professional, and merchant occupations. Manufacturers and government employees, by contrast, recorded a rise in fertility from 662 to 790 and 645 to 675 per thousand, respectively.

Among workers, the stratification of differential fertility increased between 1900 and 1915, although while laborers' fertility declined, it was still over 35 percent higher than that of any other group. At the same time, the skilled workers' fertility fell to 792 per thousand, nearly ten percent below that of any other worker category and nearly identical to that of masters and manufacturers.

In 1915, differences between specific strata had become more important than those between the wider classes. At the turn of the century, fertility had been stratified by social class; the fertility of the lowest worker group was nearly a third higher than that of the highest business class group. These differences were blurred by 1915. While the fertility of masters rose, that of skilled workers declined.

Despite the changes in differences over the sixty years, there were certain continuities in occupational fertility differentials. Divided into four strata, the rank order of the occupational groups was the same in each year examined. The new business class as a whole always had the lowest fertility, followed in order by the old business class, skilled workers, and non-skilled workers. While the magnitude of differences varied—both within and between classes—there was a fundamental stability in occupational fertility differentials.

Within this stability, the most important differences were within classes. In the business class the gap between the old and new was large in 1855, narrowed in 1900, and then increased again in 1915. Among workers, there was virtually no differential in 1855, but a large one in 1900, and an even larger one in 1915.

While occupational differences were important, economic standing also was related to fertility. In 1855, the Census reported a figure for the value of the dwelling in which the family lived. While not a perfect measure, when properly modified this figure proved to be a reliable index of relative wealth.[11]

Economic standing and fertility had a curvilinear relationship in 1855 (Table 3.3). The richest and poorest families had the fewest children,

Table 3.3. Standardized Fertility Ratio, by Economic Rank, Buffalo 1855

Economic Rank	(N)	Fertility Ratio
90–99th percentile	(897)	910
80–89th percentile	(930)	917
60–79th percentile	(2,000)	1,127
40–59th percentile	(1,733)	1,119
20–39th percentile	(1,864)	1,024
0–19th percentile	(1,714)	788

SOURCE: Calculated from New York State Census manuscripts.

while those in the middle had larger families. For example, the ratio for the richest ten percent was 910 per thousand and that of the poorest 20 percent was 788 per thousand, while the middle ranks had fertility in the 1,100 per thousand range.

At the same time, wealth and social class appear to have interacted. Among the old business class, dwelling value was positively related to fertility. From a peak of 1,169 per thousand among those in the 60–79th percentile of wealth, the fertility ratio fell to 622 per thousand among those in the bottom twenty percent. A much weaker relationship was discernable among workers; only the poorest group had a fertility ratio much lower than the group average.[12]

These data pose some interesting questions about the role of culture and economics in fertility. We might speculate that for members of the business class, deprivation was as much psychological as material. The worn rug, the frayed white collar, and perhaps the decision to limit fertility were the marks of financial constraint. Those members of the business class with middling wealth displayed signficantly lower fertility than their better-off peers.

The working class was not affected by these considerations. Virtually all groups had high fertility. Only the poorest families, exposed to extreme deprivation, had lower fertility. For the business class, deprivation was a psychological state, for workers it was a material reality.

Birthplace and Fertility

Birthplace had the strongest relationship to fertility in each of the three years for which we have evidence. In 1855, the major divide was between native-born and foreign-born families, while in later years divisions emerged among foreign-born groups.

In 1855, the largest ethnic group, the Germans, had the highest fertility (1,404 per thousand), but the Irish and Canadians then were close behind (Table 3.4). Only native-born families had a much lower ratio (930 per thousand).

At the turn of the century, while general fertility had declined, the ethnic differentials in fertility had increased. The native-born—which now included many second-generation ethnics—had a fertility ratio of 725 per thousand, a decline of over 20 percent from 1855. Germans and Irish had slightly lowered fertility, but only the Canadians had reduced their family size dramatically (32 percent).

The most striking change in 1900, however, was the presence of the new immigrant groups, all of which had fertility well above that of the older groups. The Poles' fertility ratio—1,821 per thousand—was the highest, while Italians (1,724 per thousand) and those born in Russia (1,616 per thousand) were also well above average.

These same differences were present in completed fertility (Table 3.5). Native-born couples of native parents had the fewest children (2.4), while the native-born couples of Irish and German parents had completed family sizes of 3.4 and 4.4, respectively. Among immigrants, the Irish and German figures were 3.5 and 4.1, respectively, while the average Polish couple had more than 7.5 children.

Given the demographic stability of the late nineteenth century, the changes between 1900 and 1915 are quite surprising. With the exception of the Italians, all ethnic groups' fertility fell by over one percent per year.

Table 3.4.   Standardized Fertility Ratio, by Place of Birth, Corrected for Mortality, Buffalo, 1855, 1900, 1915

Birthplace	(N)	1855	(N)	1900	(N)	1915	1855–1900	1900–1915
			Census Year				Annual Decline (%)	
United States	(1,883)	930	(2,230)	725	(3,546)	590	0.55	2.70
Canada	(201)	1,234	(191)	838	(177)	555	0.86	1.37
Ireland	(1,537)	1,368	(138)	1,198	(103)	620	0.29	4.30
Germany	(4,398)	1,404	(771)	1,250	(417)	986	0.26	1.57
Poland	—	—	(346)	1,821	(433)	1,459	—	1.47
Italy	—	—	(89)	1,724	(291)	1,640	—	0.33
Russia	—	—	(22)	1,616	(139)	1,209	—	1.92

Source: Calculated from U.S. and New York State Census manuscripts.

Table 3.5.   Estimated Children-Ever-Born at Age 50, by Ethnicity, Erie
County, 1900

Birthplace and Ethnicity	(N)	Number of Children Ever Born
Native-born		
Native-born father	(1,317)	2.43
Irish-born father	(259)	3.43
German-born father	(962)	4.39
Other	(314)	2.95
Canada	(253)	3.11
Ireland	(264)	3.48
Germany	(1,241)	4.15
Poland	(400)	7.53
Other	(531)	4.07

SOURCE: Calculated from U.S. Census manuscripts.

The Irish, Canadians, and native-born led the way, with fertility ratios
of 620, 555, and 590 per thousand, respectively, but the Germans, Poles,
and Russians also showed rapid reductions in their fertility.

Still, in relative terms, the same pattern of differential fertility was
in place. The natives and Canadians were joined by the Irish as low
fertility groups, but Germans continued to occupy a middle ground between
these groups and the new immigrants. Among the newer groups, the Poles
and Italians changed places; in 1900, the Poles had the highest fertility,
while in 1915 that honor went to the Italians.

The fertility patterns of Erie County, then, were marked by change
and continuity. Fertility declined rapidly in the population as a whole,
falling by nearly thirty percent. Most groups in the city, with the exception
of the laborers, participated in this decline.

In spite of this general decline, however, occupational and ethnic
differences persisted. The same fertility ranking of the various occupational categories was present in each year studied, although the differences
within the business class narrowed and those in the working class widened.
Among ethnic groups, the natives were at the bottom in each year, while
the relative position of the old and new immigrants remained generally
stable.

To identify patterns is not the same as explaining them. To do so,
we need to investigate more precisely the contours of fertility: the process
of decline, its economic logic, and the impact of culture and assimilation.
We turn, then, to these issues.

The Process of Decline: Innovation and Adjustment

We know that marital fertility declined significantly in Buffalo between 1855 and 1915. Some ethnic and occupational groups declined rapidly, while others declined more slowly or not at all. But what was the nature of this decline? Was the decline incremental, the steady adaptation of families to a new set of conditions? Or was it revolutionary, a sharp break with the past in attitude and behavior?

As we have seen, Wrigley and Carlsson, studying preindustrial populations, were impressed by the variability of fertility. They believed that even before the demographic transition, families knew how to restrict their fertility. The transition was a response to changing social conditions, not a change in *mentalité*.

The scholars of the European Fertility Project do not accept the argument. According to them, the pace and structure of fertility suggests that there were many economically "unwanted" births before the transition. Only a new *mentalité* and new knowledge of contraceptive techniques can explain the radical restructuring of fertility. The decline in fertility was an innovation, not an adjustment.

Since we rarely have direct evidence of couples' beliefs or their knowledge of contraception, demographers have searched for statistical means of probing these murky subjects. This task is greatly complicated by the variety of fertility experiences that have been discovered throughout the world.

The standard against which we can measure family limitation is "natural fertility," the level of fertility displayed by a population in which no fertility limitation is attempted. While the concept is simple, natural fertility varies considerably from population to population. Fecundity, foetal mortality, post-partum coital taboos, amenorrhea (the infecund period following a pregnancy), and coital frequency all have a strong impact on fertility, even in a society without conscious attempts at fertility limitation.[13]

Indeed, some attempts to control fertility are consistent with "natural fertility." Birth-spacing—the extension of the periods between births—may lower the number of children a couple has, but it does not mean that they are attempting to terminate fertility at a specific level (even if that level is high). Therefore, low fertility may occur under "natural" fertility, and high fertility with family limitation.[14]

While level of fertility is an unreliable index of family limitation, the age structure of fertility is more telling. Coale and Trussel, for example, used cross-cultural data to devise a set of measures for the degree of family limitation, based solely on the age structure of marital fertility. This statistic, which they named "m," allows demographers to estimate the degree of family limitation present in any population.[15]

To simplify, Coale and Trussel's model indicates that in societies with natural fertility, the shape of the age-specific fertility curve is convex with a late peak in fertility and a slow decline among older married women. Among contracepting populations, on the other hand, the age-specific curve peaks relatively early in the life cycle and then declines quickly among women in their late thirties and early forties. Its characteristic shape is concave.

For a number of technical reasons, we will not calculate Coale and Trussel's "m" for the Erie County data. We will, however, pay particular attention to the characteristics of family limitations—an early, high peak and a concave curve.[16]

Occupational groups displayed a variety of patterns of age-specific fertility between 1855 and 1915. Some groups moved early to a family limitation pattern, while other occupations resisted this transition. Yet the fit between a group's level of fertility and its age structure was not perfect. Particularly in the early stages of the transition, some groups lowered their fertility without its age structure changing.

Professionals and business employees were the first groups to display a limitation pattern. The business employees—although their overall fertility was higher than that of the professionals—adhered to the limitation pattern more consistently. From 1855 through 1915, the peak fertility for business employees was in the 25–29-year-old cohort, and the older cohorts' fertility diminished steeply (See Figure 3.1). Thus, the low fertility of this group was reflected in a family limitation age-pattern.

While professionals' fertility was the lowest of any occupational group in 1855, their age-specific fertility was not consistent with the family limitation pattern (See Figure 3.2). Indeed, the fertility ratio of women in the 40–44 cohort was virtually the same as that of women in their late twenties and thirties in 1855.

By contrast, in 1900, professionals' wives aged 25–29 actually had higher fertility than their counterparts in 1855, but their fertility at other ages was much lower. For older women in 1900, fertility dropped abruptly—

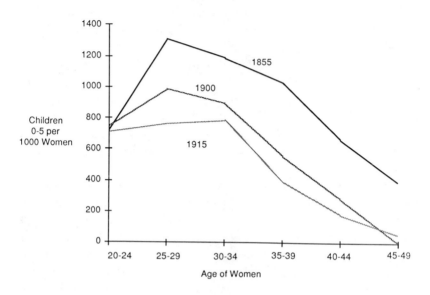

Figure 3.1
Age-specific Fertility Ratios,
Business Employees
Erie County, 1855, 1900, 1915

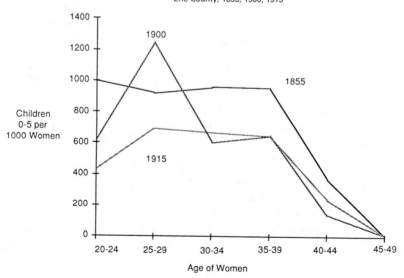

Figure 3.2
Age-specific Fertility Ratios,
Professionals,
Erie County, 1855, 1900, 1915

from 1,247 per thousand for women ages 25–29 to 604 and 651 per thousand for women in the 30–34 and 35–39 age cohorts, respectively. By 1915, their overall fertility had again fallen as women in their twenties reduced their fertility.

The professionals and business employees were the pioneers of fertility decline in Buffalo. Yet they moved to lower fertility in different ways. The professionals began with an age-specific pattern that was similar to that of other business groups and only moved to a limitation pattern in the late nineteenth century. The business employees, although their fertility was higher than that of professionals, exhibited a family limitation pattern earlier.

Merchants and agents displayed little evidence of the family limitation pattern during our study (Figure 3.3). In all years, they had high fertility in the 30–34 age cohort. When they did lower fertility, they did so by restricting births throughout the life cycle, among 20–24 year old women as well as older cohorts. Spacing—not family limitation—most likely was their initial means of limiting fertility.

Masters and manufacturers, by comparison, moved decisively to a family limitation pattern in the early twentieth century (Figure 3.4). In 1855, they displayed a traditional pattern of a flat, convex age-specific fertility curve, but by 1900, they had an early peak and a concave curve.

The old business class continued to display diversity in fertility patterns. For example, by 1900, Joseph Zahn, a merchant, and his wife Mary had had twelve children in their 34 years of marriage, and saloon-keeper John Oitner and his wife Louisa, in 19 years of marriage, had had eight children. On the other hand, the manufacturer Morris Diamond and his wife Nellie had two children in the first 3 years of their marriage, but then had only one daughter in the next 7 years.

The new business class, on the other hand, had become much more homogeneous by 1900. Harriet Duke, the wife of a bakery manager, had borne only one child in 32 years of marriage; Harriet Fleming and her journalist husband had had no children in 19 years of marriage; and Mary Jones, the wife of a physician, was also childless. Large families had become rare among professionals and business employees.

The working class adopted family limitation more slowly. In 1855, the skilled workers' fertility curve was heavily convex (Figure 3.5). The age-specific fertility ratio was low only among women in their forties. By the early twentieth century, however, an early peak and a rapid decline during the thirties was common. Transport workers, too, moved toward

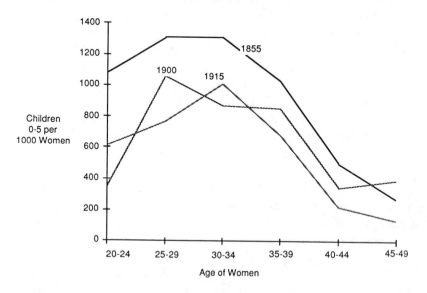

Figure 3.3
Age-specific Fertility Ratios,
Merchants and Agents,
Erie County, 1855, 1900, 1915

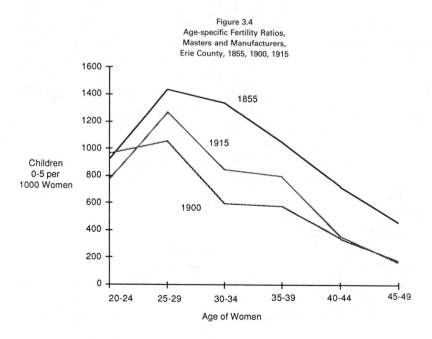

Figure 3.4
Age-specific Fertility Ratios,
Masters and Manufacturers,
Erie County, 1855, 1900, 1915

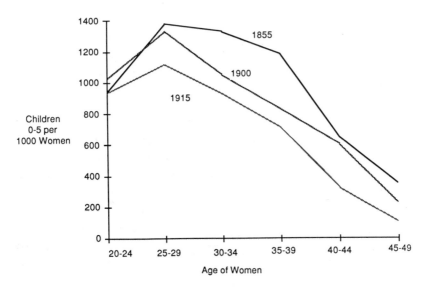

Figure 3.5
Age-specific Fertility Ratios,
Skilled Workers,
Erie County, 1855, 1900, 1915

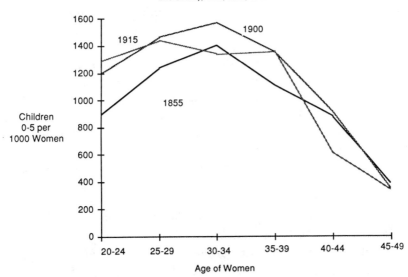

Figure 3.6
Age-specific Fertility Ratios,
Laborers,
Erie County, 1855, 1900, 1915

a new pattern in the early twentieth century. In 1855 and 1900, the age structure of fertility for this group was virtually flat, but in 1915, their age-specific ratio peaked among women in their late twenties and went down steeply among older women.

Laborers consistently had the highest fertility in the city. As expected, they showed few signs of adopting family limitation (Figure 3.6). In 1855 and 1900, their highest age-specific ratio was among women aged 30–34, while even in 1915, the age-specific curve was essentially flat between the ages of 20 and 39.

Each stratum of Erie County's occupational structure moved toward lower fertility in a different way. The new business class moved decisively to adopt family limitation; although they had small families in 1855, it wasn't until 1900 that a clear pattern of family limitation was obvious. The old business class was more wedded to the old pattern; even when their fertility dropped in the early twentieth century, they did not show a clear pattern of limitation. Like the old business class, skilled workers moved toward declining fertility and family limitation toward 1900. Finally, unskilled workers retained high fertility and a traditional age-specific pattern.

The ethnic groups of the city, too, exhibited great variety in their levels and patterns of fertility. Some groups—the natives and Canadians— had low fertility and a family-limitation pattern as early as 1855. The Germans, in contrast, passed through the transition both in level and age pattern between 1855 and 1915. Finally, the later immigrants retained a more traditional age pattern of fertility even while their level of fertility dropped between 1900 and 1915. (Figures 3.7–3.12).

The Irish, however, had the most distinctive pattern. While Irish fertility was consistently lower than that of the Germans, they showed no signs of adopting family limitation. Rather, the data suggest that child spacing—a reduced level of fertility across the woman's life cycle—was popular among the Irish. In none of the three census years did their age-specific fertility ratio decline before the age of 40.

To what extent was this distinctive pattern a product of the unique Irish historical experience? In the wake of the potato famine, Ireland was one of the first western nations to limit its fertility. Indeed, the combination of low fertility and high out-migration caused Ireland's total population to decline from 1840 until after the turn of the century. However, the Irish did not reduce their fertility by limiting marital fertility. The fertility

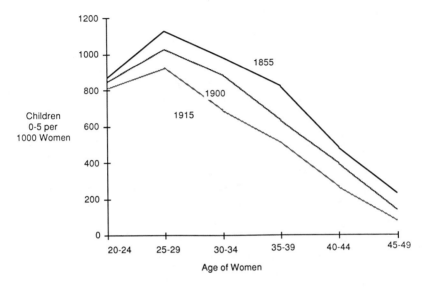

Figure 3.7
Age-specific Fertility Ratios,
Native-born,
Erie County, 1855, 1900, 1915

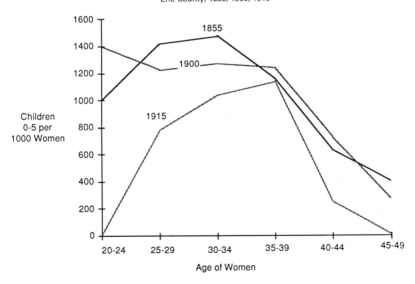

Figure 3.8
Age-specific Fertility Ratios,
Irish-born,
Erie County, 1855, 1900, 1915

transition did not begin in Ireland until 1929, the latest of any European nation. The island's low total fertility was the result, rather, of the low marriage rate.[17]

The Irish-Americans of Erie County, too, did not appear to adopt family limitation. Yet they did find some way to reduce their overall level of marital fertility. They most likely accomplished this by spacing their children across the life cycle.

Other minor ethnic differences are worth noting. In 1900, among natives of foreign ancestry, those of Irish background resembled the Irish-born—a flat age-pattern with little decline—while the women of German ancestry, unlike the German-born, exhibited a family limitation pattern. Finally, among the new immigrants, only the Russian-born stood out because their overall fertility was lower (Figures 3.8–3.12).

The analysis of age-specific fertility confirms many of the conclusions drawn from earlier data. Those groups with the lowest level of fertility usually also had a family-limitation pattern of age-specific fertility. We should not ignore, however, those cases in which there was not a good fit between these two factors. The professionals' age-fertility pattern in 1855, for example, was not that of limiting births in spite of their low level of fertility. Similarly, the masters and skilled workers moved to lower over-all fertility before they adopted a family-limitation age pattern. Finally, the Irish had a distinctive pattern that showed no indication of family limitation.

The Erie County data suggest that true family limitation was an innovation in family strategy. When groups shifted to lower fertility, the change in its age-specific fertility was usually dramatic. The new business class, the Germans, the skilled and transport workers, all went through this transition between 1855 and 1915. In general, these data confirm the innovative character of the fertility decline.

Yet there was a lag between the decline of fertility and the adoption of the family-limitation fertility pattern. Among several groups, a more traditional method of fertility restriction—child spacing—appears to have been used early in the transition. Erie County's families apparently had ways of restricting fertility before they adopted more modern practices.

The old methods, however, were of limited value. They might help *begin* the fertility transition, but they were not effective enough to complete it. As couples decided to limit fertility they looked for and discovered new techniques.

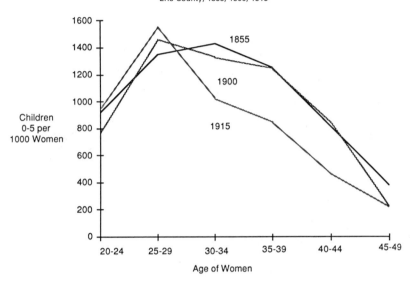

Figure 3.9
Age-specific Fertility Ratios,
German-born,
Erie County, 1855, 1900, 1915

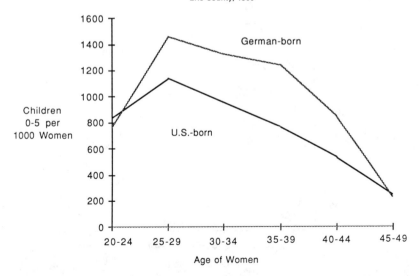

Figure 3.10
Age-specific Fertility Ratios,
German Ancestry,
Erie County, 1900

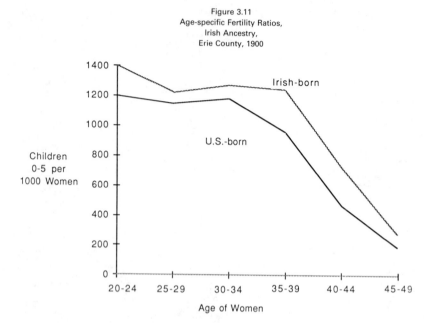

Figure 3.11
Age-specific Fertility Ratios,
Irish Ancestry,
Erie County, 1900

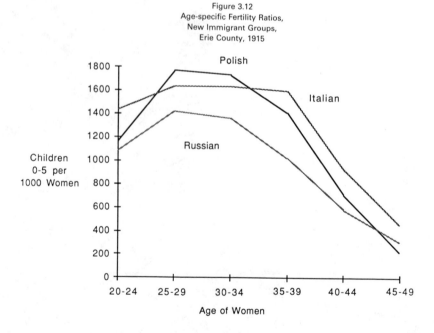

Figure 3.12
Age-specific Fertility Ratios,
New Immigrant Groups,
Erie County, 1915

These data, then, give some support to each position. They confirm Knodel and van de Walle's assertion that family limitation—characterized by an early peak and rapid decline in age-specific fertility—represented an historic break with pretransition patterns. On the other hand, with Wrigley and Carlsson, the data suggest that there was an earlier pattern of birth control associated with longer birth intervals and a suppressed level of fertility across the women's life cycle.[18]

The results dispute the claim that families went from no knowledge of family limitation to the modern pattern. Rather, it appears that the fertility transition sometimes occurred in two stages. As families decided to restrict fertility, they first employed the older methods of prolonging the period between births. When these methods proved unable to achieve the desired results, families sought new strategies more consistent with the modern family-limitation model. The decline of fertility may have been a more subtle combination of continuity and discontinuity than we have appreciated.

The process of fertility decline may also tell us something about how social and cultural change occurs. The first response to changing conditions among the families of Erie County was to adopt older patterns of behavior. But when these patterns proved inadequate, they fell apart, and individuals had to find new, more effective responses. While this three-stage model—old condition/old patterns, new conditions/old patterns, new conditions/new patterns—provides a means of conceptualizing the interaction of cultural and social change, we must still investigate the timing of the transition.

The ability to ferret out these patterns is, to some extent, a result of our methods. The aggregate data employed by most demographers would make it extremely difficult to identify the transitional use of traditional methods that our findings suggest.

These results, in addition, underline the importance of class and ethnicity. If not disaggregated, the sharpness of the shift from one pattern to another is obscured. The fertility transition was really a combination of a whole set of smaller transitions, as the population—group by group—changed the way it thought about family size. While a longer view may make the patterns more straightforward, it may hide the complexity and significance of the experience.

We have now investigated the contours of the fertility transition in Erie County and the process through which it occurred. Yet, we still don't understand why it happened. To address this issue, two topics must be considered: the logic of family limitation, and its cultural meaning.

The Logic of Fertility Decline

The analysis of age-specific data suggest that the fertility transition represented cultural innovation: the decline of fertility was the result of new behaviors and attitudes. But not all groups went through this transition at the same time. Some occupational and ethnic groups restricted their family sizes early, while others lagged behind.

What was the cause of this lag? Historical demographers have generally used one or the other of two possible explanations. For some, the protracted transition was caused by the slow change in economic conditions. Others have focused not on economics but on the slow diffusion of innovations. For scholars of the first school of thought, the explanation of fertility differentials lies in the uneven spread of industrialization and of rising standards of living, while the second set of scholars focuses on the relative cultural backwardness of some groups and their resistance to change.

An explanation of fertility that ignores either structural or cultural change is doomed to failure. Social structure is not "a simple reflex, a 'mirror image' " of culture, nor vice versa. Rather, following Geertz, we must "distinguish analytically between cultural and social aspects of human life, and . . . treat them as independently variable yet mutually interdependent factors."[19]

In the case of fertility, we can do this by following Lesthaeghe's analytical division between the cost/benefit logic that governed the fertility decline and the cultural processes—social control and socialization—that resisted such change. Therefore, in this section, we examine how the economic context in which Erie County's families lived influenced their family limitation decisions. Then, in the following section, we turn to the cultural dimensions of fertility decline.

However, Lesthaeghe's conceptualization is flawed by the data on which it is based. The fertility transition was really a series of mini-transitions, as different social classes and ethnic groups reduced their fertility. Therefore, to study the cost/benefit of fertility, we must examine the specific conditions of each social stratum and how those conditions influenced the decision to limit fertility.

The Family Strategy of the Business Class

The key to the alteration of the business class's family strategy was the transformation of bourgeois property. In the strictly entrepreneurial economy, a father's property passed to the son, whatever his personal qualities. Bright or stupid, quick or slow, he was still the boss's son and heir.

The centrality of this relationship to commercial capitalism was noted by Joseph Schumpeter:

> The family and the family home used to be the mainspring of the typically bourgeois kind of profit motive. Economists have not always given due weight to this fact. When we look more closely at their idea of the self-interest of entrepreneurs and capitalists we cannot fail to discover that the results it was supposed to produce are really not at all what one would expect from the rational self-interest of the detached individual or the childless couple who no longer look at the world through the windows of a family home. Consciously or unconsciously they analyzed the behavior of the man whose views and motives are shaped by a home and who means to work and to save primarily for wife and children.[20]

The nature of inheritance also influenced the type and level of family expenditure. The required costs of child-rearing were relatively low. The most important training—the skill required to manage men and machines—was learned in the normal operation of business. The countinghouse and shop floor were the schools of the old business class.

The late nineteenth-century concentration of business ownership attacked this family economy. Certainly, life-chances were better than average even if one's father were merely a manager or head clerk, but thenature of this occupational and status inheritance was radically different.

Objective qualifications and formal education had become the arbiters of occupational mobility. First for the professions and then for business employees, education became the great switchinghouse in which a youth's status and fate were decided.

"The most attractive new jobs," according to Joseph Kett, were in the white collar sector, in which, "education to age 14 and preferably to 16 or 18," was a requirement. While earlier in the century, "class differences had not been reflected primarily in the early and middle teens," by the late nineteenth century, "middle class parents had to adopt a different strategy, that of placing children in their early teens on the track of formal education."[21]

This was not the only social force affecting the logic of business-class family life. At the same time that parents began to spend more on their children, the new consumer society demanded that they spend more on themselves.

A business class—splintered by structural changes in the economy—used consumption patterns to pull itself together again. Members of the old and new business class used a similar standard of living to affirm their common class position and to distinguish themselves from the working class. Suddenly, considerations of status and leisure demanded a greater share of the family budget.

It is no coincidence that the turn of the century produced Thorstein Veblen's analysis of the leisure class, as well as concerns among more popular writers about the role of leisure in the life of business people. Summer vacations became more common after 1850 and a "campaign against national feverishness," according to Daniel Rodgers, decried "the hectic pace of brain workers" and "the burdens of middle-class living."[22]

The bookkeeper or plant manager could no longer aspire to ownership and had relatively little control over directing the business. Still, in an era in which the "problem of production" had given way to an abundant society, he could be assured that "invidious" distinctions of conspicuous consumption differentiated him from the company's work hands.

The timing of expenditures also had to change. The ideal of the sober clerk—postponing consumption to accumulate his "competence"—passed into folklore. While consumerism did not become a mass phenomenon until the 1920s, the philosophy of "buy now—pay later" had penetrated Middletown by the turn of the century.[23]

A crisis was in the making. On the one hand, the logic of child rearing encouraged the new business class to spend more heavily on its children and to prolong their education. At the same time, the changing cultural definition of the business class forced its members to spend more on their own standard of living.

It was this crisis of family life that caused so much worry on the part of popular writers. Part of the answer to it lay in cultural change—like the redefinition of the work ethic described by Rodgers.[24] Another answer was to change the family strategy of the business class and to limit its fertility.

The professionals and business employees of the new business class were the first to change. Yet, other business families were not immune to the same logic. The organization of production and the white-collar job market were not stable. As the nineteenth century drew to a close, old-business-class parents found fewer opportunities open in family firms. Management and the professions were the paths of mobility for their sons. By the turn of the century, the old business class, too, sent its children to school longer and restricted its own fertility.

Strong forces, then, were weighing on the business class. Caldwell's net flow of wealth influenced the direction of fertility. This consideration shared the stage, however, with concerns over social standing and status transmission.

For the families of new business class, these two influences reinforced one another. Since their only strategy for guaranteeing their children's future was increased education, they had a double incentive to limit fertility. Caldwell's "compass swing" was consistent with status concerns. As new business class parents accommodated themselves to the new realities of the opportunity structure, they led the movement to lower fertility.

The old business class was in a more ambiguous position. For its members, the imperatives of transferring their status were less clear-cut. They could choose either to spend more on education and prepare their children for the world of the white-collar worker or continue to place them in entrepreneurial positions. The two factors—net income flows and status concerns—worked at cross-purposes and slowed the decline of fertility.

Late in the century, however, as the incorporation of the economy accelerated, the entrepreneurial option looked less and less promising, and the old business class shifted to a new family strategy. Still, some segments of it—particularly the large immigrant commercial stratum—resisted the change; their fertility did not plummet, but drifted down.

Like the story of the tortoise and the hare, business-class fertility strategies diverged and then came together. The professionals and business employees moved decisively to reduce their fertility around midcentury. Then, later in the century, the older stratum of the business class—slowly but steadily—adopted a smaller family.

The American situation was similar to that facing the British middle classes at midcentury, a story already brilliantly told by J. A. Banks. According to Banks, the fertility decline in England was caused by the squeeze placed on middle-class incomes by the Great Depression of the 1870s. While other historians have questioned the timing in Banks's argument (the decline began before families felt the full weight of the Depression), his explanation of the structural situation of the Victorian middle class remains convincing.[25]

Banks's argument, however, is less persuasive for the working class. According to Banks, workers lowered their fertility as they adopted middle-class norms through a process of cultural diffusion. Yet, while we cannot minimize the role of culture, if social structural forces were important for middle-class fertility, it stands to reason that they were also important for the working class.

The Family Strategy of the Working Class

As the working class divided at the turn of the century, those families in the secondary stratum—still subject to poverty, unemployment, and disruption—clung to an old family strategy. In contrast, a new set of opportunities opened for those families in the primary sector. For the first time, this stratum could escape the poverty and uncertainty that were the basis of working class life in the nineteenth century.

A number of scholars have already identified the contours of the working-class's old family strategy. The husband's income was usually insufficient to support the family. Children left school early and entered the labor force to supplement family income. Although wives rarely worked for wages, boarding was a common means of increasing income. Property ownership often served as a defense against the twin threats of unemployment and old age.[26]

The linchpin of this family strategy was poverty. As Steven Dubnoff has discovered, the working class's standard of living in 1890, even after decades of economic growth, was "very close to bare subsistence." Dubnoff found that for a couple marrying in 1870, the average male income remained below adequacy for twenty years of the family's life cycle. In addition, this average working-class family's income was only three-fourths of adequacy for over a decade. Thus, even for those families not totally indigent, poverty was a predictable element of working-class experience.[27]

The level of working-class income during the late nineteenth century did not only set a limit on material expenditures; it limited the scope and horizon of planning, as well. Although poverty was predictable, its timing, duration, and severity were not. Without a predictable pattern of work or employment, long-term planning was futile. "Short-term crisis management" was the "rational" orientation of the working class.[28]

The segmentation of the working class and its rising standards of living changed this situation. The average working-class couple who married in 1900, according to Dubnoff, would slip below income adequacy for fifteen years—five years shorter than the same couple thirty years earlier. More significantly, its income would only fall below three-fourths of adequacy for two years—less than one-fifth of the period for the earlier cohort. In one generation, the spectre of poverty for the average working class family had begun to vanish.

In the Buffalo of 1918, while the lower tier of the working class—laborers and transport workers—continued to live in deprivation, the upper tier of factory and skilled workers had risen out of poverty. These better-off workers were no longer the impoverished proletariat of the nineteenth-century city. They represented the first concrete embodiment of the much ballyhooed "American standard of living."[29]

The social context of working-class life, too, was altered by the decline in poverty. In England, Gareth Stedman Jones found that the working class was "remade" in the early twentieth century. A "culture of consolation" replaced the assertive working-class culture of the early nineteenth century. "The main impetus of working class activity now lay elsewhere," according to Stedman Jones. "It concentrated into trade unions, co-ops, friendly societies, all indicating a *de facto* recognition of the existing social order as the inevitable framework of action."[30]

The "culture of consolation" was not identical in Britain and the United States. The contours of American society—the vitality of the economy and heavy immigration—had created a working class that was less united and self-conscious. Yet, for the workers of the primary stratum, a number of forces contributed to a new working-class culture, more integrated in (or at least more accepting of) the dominant social order.

The nuclear family increased in importance. The boundaries of the family household in the nineteenth century had been permeable. Boarders and lodgers entered freely, other relatives were common, and youths left early to live in other families. Where possible, broad kin networks served to cushion the jolts of the early industrial economy.[31]

For the new working class, the interaction of a rising standard of living and the changing opportunity structure shifted the calculus of family economy. Increased family incomes combined with an improved clerical job market and vocational training to encourage increased schooling. Less likely to need the aid of other family members, well-off working families were more likely to use their resources to advance the prospects of their children and to improve their current standard of living.

At the end of the nineteenth century, few working-class youths entered white-collar jobs. According to Clyde and Sally Griffen, the paths of mobility between manual and mental work had closed after 1850. At midcentury, skilled workers often moved into business occupations; but by the 1880s, clerks—often the sons of entrepreneurs—had become the primary source of recruits to the commercial occupations.[32]

Schooling had little use in this context. Small wonder that the youths of Hamilton, Ontario, according to Katz and Davey, used the city's schools as little more than a haven from a bad job market. Conditions dictated a strategy of early labor force entry in the hope of acquiring the knowledge, connections, or capital needed for mobility.[33]

At the same time that the standards of living of the working class were changing, the calculus for schooling was transformed as well. On the one hand, the availability of youth work declined, leaving young people without job prospects; on the other hand, clerical opportunities increased, encouraging them to stay in school longer for vocational training.

"The crucial elements of the modern institutional structure were put into place at the turn of the century," according to Paul Osterman. "Youths left the labor market and stayed in school longer. Child labor and compulsory education laws were strengthened and extended, and the high school became a mass institution." Compulsory education and child-labor laws dried up the supply of child labor at the same time that technological change was lowering the demand for it. As Musgrove noted for England: "Young people were no longer central to the economy."[34]

Simultaneously, opportunities in the world of the office exploded. In Buffalo, we should recall, the number of business employees and professionals nearly doubled between 1900 and 1915. Nationally, the trend was even more impressive; the number of clerical jobs increased from 3.1 to 8.1 percent of the labor force between 1900 and 1920.[35]

As this stratum expanded, the opportunities for working-class youths improved. Jane Synge, for example, found that equal proportions of working- and business-class women entered clerical work in Hamilton, Ontario, in the early twentieth century. Similarly, C. Wright Mills found that in the 1930s and 1940s about half of white-collar workers were the children of wage-earners. Education was a prerequisite for these new jobs.[36]

The families of the working class found themselves facing a new reality in the first years of this century. The grey nineteenth-century world of misery and privation gave way to a modest prosperity. The new opportunities that accompanied this progress shifted the logic of working-class life. The old family strategy of boarding, child labor, and extended kin gave way to a new calculus. The net flow of wealth shifted from parents to children. Children consumed more and entered the labor force later. The working class had crossed Caldwell's "great divide."

Social Structure and Culture

While the fertility transition would not have occurred without a radical change in the context and economy of family life, to focus only on these structural issues ignores the complexity of the fertility transition. While the restructuring of the labor market, the increased importance of education, and the decline in poverty all had important influences on fertility, these were qualified, limited, and altered by cultural influences.

This is hardly surprising. When social action is under individual control, perception, the definition of the situation, and the meaning attached to social action will influence what happens. Since fertility is, after all, usually one of the most privately controlled social actions, we cannot understand it without grasping its cultural dimension.

The most striking cultural split in nineteenth- and early twentieth-century Erie County was the one between the native-born and the immigrants. While native American culture was itself going through changes during this period—becoming "incorporated," in Alan Trachtenberg's phrase—these shifts were less dramatic than those experienced by immigrants and their children.[37]

Immigrants retained a commitment to high fertility even after the native-born began to limit family size. Yet, the label "ethnic culture" does little to illuminate the nature or process through which these families forged their fertility strategies. Was high fertility simply the irrational hold of folk culture and superstition, or was the fertility behavior of immigrants lodged in a set of beliefs that they did not share with the native-born but which had its own rationality?

We must cast our net more widely to penetrate this question. In the next chapter, we will investigate the history of schooling and its impact on fertility. Here, we wish to focus on the process through which immigrants moved toward lower fertility. Four kinds of evidence inform this discussion: class differentials within immigrant groups, intergenerational fertility, the impact of exogamy, and the relationship of fertility and migration.

Class and Ethnicity

Erie County's fertility was marked by clear occupational and ethnic differentials. Each occupational stratum moved toward lower fertility at its own pace, and ethnic differences were the strongest influence on fertility in each of the years we are examining.

These factors could be related in two ways. First, because they are *correlated*, the simple computations we have examined so far overstate the independent influence of each. Since families in low-fertility occupational groups were more likely to be in low-fertility ethnic groups, controlling for these factors reduces the relationship of each to fertility. Second, ethnicity and occupation could *interact*, that is, the ethnic distribution of each occupational group could be different (or vice versa).[38]

The data from Erie County suggest that when we control for the two variables, the influence of each is reduced (Table 3.6). Because occupation and ethnicity are correlated, the ethnic differentials within each stratum are less than those in the entire population. Yet, with a few exceptions, the two variables had independent influences on fertility.

The split between the fertility of the two business-class strata was present among ethnic groups in all three years. For example, among Germans in 1855, the fertility of the new business class (877 per thousand) was far lower than that of either the old business class (1,285 per thousand) or the working class (1,081 per thousand). Although the differences between the new business class and the other strata were not as dramatic among the Irish, the new business-class ratio of 1,028 was substantially below that of the other two strata. Finally, among natives, the new business stratum had lower fertility than either other stratum.

The same generalization is true in 1900 and 1915: clear class differentials were present in all ethnic groups. For example, among German-born in 1900, the new business class's fertility ratio (729 per thousand) was substantially below that of the old business class (906 per thousand), which in turn was below that of either working class group. In 1915, the differences between the two business strata were present among all ethnic groups except the Poles.

Table 3.6. Standardized Fertility Ratios, by Occupation and Birthplace, Erie County, 1855, 1900, 1915

Birthplace	Old Business Class	New Business Class	Working Class	
1855				
United States	795	711	766	
Canada	1,073	720	987	
Ireland	1,070	1,028	1,124	
Germany	1,285	877	1,081	
1900			Skilled Workers	Other Workers
United States	551	539	714	746
Canada	630	460	836	834
Germany	906	729	1,085	1,107
Poland	1,378	1,366	1,436	1,553
1915				
United States	476	453	593	672
Canada	531	479	441	683
Germany	739	374	775	906
Austria-Hungary	1,191	680	1,236	1,231
Poland	942	1,506	1,314	1,262
Italy	1,489	1,208	1,346	1,367
Russia	883	607	1,231	1,279

SOURCE: Calculated from U.S. and New York State Census manuscripts.
NOTE: 1855 data is for Buffalo only.

The emerging difference between the two strata of the working class, however, was less consistent. In 1900, native- and German-born skilled workers had marginally lower fertility than "other workers," but only the Poles had a dramatic difference between skilled and nonskilled workers (1,436 vs. 1,553 per thousand). In 1915, the skilled workers' fertility was lower than that of other manual workers for all groups except the Austro-Hungarians and the Poles. Still, among the other new immigrant groups, these differentials were quite small: 21 per thousand for Italians and 48 per thousand for the Russian-born. Labor market segmentation was correlated with fertility for the native-born and old immigrant groups, but not for the new immigrants.

The uniqueness of the new immigrants is worth noting. Except for those from Russia, these groups were primarily in the secondary stratum of the working class. While some struggled to gain more secure employment, many wished to work only for a few years and then return to their homelands. Therefore, we will need to explore migration history and life cycle to gain a fuller understanding of these groups' fertility.

At the same time, each occupational stratum had strong ethnic differences. In 1855, the fertility ratios of the working class ranged from 766 per thousand among the native-born to 1,124 per thousand for the Irish. Similarly, in 1915, the new business class's ratios ranged from 374 per thousand for Germans to 1,506 for the Poles.

While birthplace and social class were correlated, their relationships to fertility were independent. Compared to members of the new business class from other ethnic groups, a German-born professional had the high fertility of a German, but compared to other German-born, he acted like a member of the new business class.[39]

Intergenerational Differences

The children of immigrants did not retain their parents' fertility strategy. In 1900, the only year for which we have data on parents' birthplace, the fertility of all second-generation Americans in Buffalo was lower than that of immigrants (Table 3.7). For example, American-born of German parents had a fertility ratio nearly thirty percent lower than that of German-born couples. The differences between Irish-born couples and American-born couples of Irish ancestry was nearly twenty percent.

The only exception to this pattern was the British, whose second-generation fertility was only slightly below that of British immigrants. Of

Table 3.7. Standardized Fertility Ratio, by Ethnicity and Immigrant Status, Erie County, 1900

Ethnicity	(N)	Immigrant Status		
		Immigrant	(N)	Native-Born
Canada	(191)	728	(35)	724
Ireland	(138)	1,048	(259)	879
Germany	(771)	1,050	(831)	770
England and Wales	(154)	664	(135)	630
All natives			(2,230)	669
Native-born of native parents			(1,317)	541

SOURCE: Calculated from U.S. Census manuscripts.

course, by the turn of the century, the decline in national fertility was well underway in Great Britain, so it is likely that it was not acculturation to American ways that accounted for the low fertility of this group. Still, for other groups, the fertility of second-generation Americans was substantially higher than that of families whose parents had been born in the United States, suggesting that ethnicity continued to play a role for the second generation.

As already noted, the patterns of age-specific fertility were consistent with these findings. Those born of native parents displayed both the lowest overall fertility level and the most distinctive pattern of family limitation; their fertility peaked in the 25–29 age cohort and went down steeply for older women. The second-generation German-Americans, while having higher fertility overall, also displayed such a family limitation pattern. The contrast between them and the German-born was particularly noteworthy.

The native-born of Irish ancestry were the exception to this pattern. While having lower fertility overall, their age pattern was quite similar to that of the Irish-born (Figure 3.11). Their age-specific fertility was relatively flat until age 35, suggesting little use of family limitation. Yet by some means the Irish were able to space their births in order to reduce overall family size.

Are the first- and second-generation fertility differentials simply a product of the improved occupational status of second-generation immigrants? The data suggest they were not. Among the old business group, the Irish immigrants and second-generation Irish had fertility ratios of 874 and 749 per thousand, while for Germans the figures were 906 and 646. Among non-skilled workers, the immigrant and the second-generation fertility comparisons were 1,156 and 747 per thousand for the Irish and 1,107 and 924 per thousand for the Germans.

In 1915, mixed marriages affected fertility as well (Table 3.8). Dividing the population into four groups—natives (including Canadians), British (including Irish), Germans, and Southern and Eastern Europeans—those couples who crossed these ethnic lines to marry had a fertility ratio between those of the two groups from which they came. Endogamous native couples had the lowest fertility, while British/British and British/American couples had a fertility ratio of 649 per thousand, about ten percent higher than the American/American couples.

Germans with either an American or British spouse also had low fertility—652 per thousand—much below that of endogamous Germans

Table 3.8. Standardized Fertility Ratio, by Couple's Birthplaces, Erie
County, 1915

Couple's Birthplaces	(N)	Fertility Ratio
United States or Canada/United States or Canada	(3,528)	543
British or Irish/US, Canada, British, or Irish	(343)	649
Germany/Germany	(226)	1,082
Germany/US, Canadian, British, or Irish	(267)	656
Germany/South or East Europe	(19)	1,132
South or East Europe/South or East Europe	(888)	1,219
Other	(240)	902

SOURCE: Calculated from New York State Census manuscripts.

(1,082 per thousand). Finally, Southern and Eastern Europeans were
almost entirely endogamous; only 19 couples with only one Southern or
Eastern European partner were present in our sample. Still, these families
had a fertility ratio between that of endogamous Germans and Southern
or Eastern Europeans.

Again, age-specific fertility analysis confirms these findings. Those
Americans, Canadians, and British (including Irish) who had married
one another, all displayed early peaks and quick declines in fertility. This
was true as well among Germans who had a spouse from one of these
groups—the peak fertility was 1,398 per thousand among women 25–29
years of age and was followed by sharp declines in successively older age
cohorts: 695, 603, and 382 per thousand, respectively. To the extent that
intermarriage was an index of acculturation, it was correlated with lower
fertility.

Migration History

The migration history of individuals can tell us a number of things.
First, if they had been in the United States a long time, we know they
had been exposed to American society and probably were not planning
to return to Europe. Second, if they migrated early in their life cycle, we
can infer that they were partially socialized in an American setting. To
differentiate these two factors, we will use two different measures of migration: length of residence and life-cycle stage of migration.[40]

Length of residence had a strong relationship to fertility in 1855 (Table 3.9). The families whose head had lived in the city between five and nineteen years had the highest fertility, while new and long-time residents had lower fertility. Controlling for occupation and ethnicity confirms the independent significance of this relationship.

At midcentury, migration was closely correlated with property-ownership. Among newcomers to the city (less than one year), owning property had little impact on fertility—the difference between owners and renters was less than one percent. Among successive migration cohorts, however, the fertility edge of renters over owners increased from 11 percent, for those resident in the city between one and four years, to 17 percent among those who had lived in the city over twenty years.

Homeownership and migration had a special relationship in the nineteenth-century city. As social historians have discovered, nineteenth-century America was a nation on the move; rarely did half the residents of a city remain from one decade to the next.[41]

The only variable that was consistently related to persistence in a community was homeownership. In a primitive land market, without easily available mortgages, only those families who were most assured of their stability would buy a home. Persistence and homeownership represented a special dimension of the social experience in nineteenth-century America, separate from the influence of social class or wealth.[42]

In Buffalo, the interaction of homeownership and persistence was related to fertility. While long-term residents in general were more likely to have low fertility, it was particularly those who owned homes, the most stable of the stable, who had the fewest children.

Life-cycle stage had an important impact on fertility, as well (Table 3.10). Those who were married before migrating to Buffalo had

Table 3.9. Standardized Fertility Ratio, by Length of Residence, Buffalo, 1855

Length of Residence	(N)	Fertility Ratio
Under 1 year	(559)	746
1–4 years	(3,068)	885
5–9 years	(2,719)	1,111
10–14 years	(1,099)	1,157
15–19 years	(683)	1,071
20 years and over	(1,061)	957

SOURCE: Calculated from New York State Census manuscripts.

Table 3.10. Standardized Fertility Ratio, by Migration, and Marital Status, Occupation, and Birthplace, Buffalo, 1855

	Born or Raised in Erie County	Migrated As Adult into Erie County	
		Married	Single
Total Population	1,000	1,109	985
(N)	(1,176)	(3,734)	(3,679)
Occupational Stratum			
Old business class	1,220	1,003	1,006
New business class	626	914	718
Working class	1,217	1,148	1,013
Other	1,020	1,078	929
Birthplace			
United States	843/643[a]	903	700
Canada	927	1,083	790
Ireland	1,072	1,198	939
Germany	1,435	1,124	984
Other	946	1,096	762

SOURCE: Calculated from New York State Census manuscripts.
[a]Born in Erie County/Raised in Erie County.

the highest current fertility, while those families headed by a man who was either born or raised or had migrated to Erie County as a single adult had much lower fertility.

This pattern was not an artifact of the age structure of the population. Not only was the fertility of those who had married in Buffalo higher in the 20–24 year age cohort, it was higher across the woman's life cycle.

Nor did ethnicity and social class significantly affect this pattern. Those who had migrated as married adults had the highest fertility whether they had been born in the United States, Ireland, or Canada, or were employed in the business or working class. Only the Germans did not conform to this pattern.

Comparisons across ethnic groups highlight the significance of life cycle. In spite of the enormous ethnic group differentials, native couples who migrated to Buffalo after they had married had a fertility ratio only five percent below that of an Irish couple who migrated before marriage or of a Canadian couple raised in Buffalo. Ethnicity was not a single variable, but a number of statuses—some cultural, others structural—rolled into one.

Consider the meaning of migration in the context of the nineteenth-century city. Community studies have made clear that at midcentury transiency was a pervasive fact of social life. Although there were differences in persistence rates, members of all groups—rich and poor, businessman and worker, native and foreigner—were likely to move, searching for better opportunities or escaping from intolerable situations. As Katz, Doucet, and Stern concluded: "a massive and continuous flow of population was one side of a coin whose reverse image was a rigid, sharply etched structure of inequality."[43]

Because migration was so common it had little group impact on fertility. Different occupational and ethnic groups did not share a common migration experience. Migration served, rather, to individualize fertility experience. It weakened social control over fertility.

While the evidence is fragile, it is possible that migration had assumed a different meaning by the early twentieth century. Transiency and insecurity became structural elements of the labor market, reinforcing the low pay and bad working conditions of the secondary stratum of the working class. Thus, migration became more closely linked to the opportunity structure, and so influenced fertility in new ways.

Because migration was linked to labor market structure, it reinforced the group identification of the new immigrants who composed the bulk of the secondary stratum. Polish factory workers, Italian laborers, and Russian craftsmen shared a common labor market position and migration history with their countrymen. This experience served to unite them and to differentiate them from other groups.

In the short term, this convergence of ethnicity, occupation, and migration reinforced the group identification of individuals and strengthened traditional moral control. While nineteenth-century migration had contributed to individuation, in the early twentieth century it may have increased group control over individual behavior, including fertility.

In 1900 and 1915, immigrants who had been in the United States between 10 and 14 years had the highest fertility of any migration cohort (Table 3.11). For example, in 1900, the fertility of those who had migrated less than five years earlier was 900 per thousand. This rose to 1,208 and 1,329 for those who had been in the United States for 5–9 and 10–14 years, respectively, and then fell to 1,156, 940, and 830 per thousand for successive migration cohorts.

The fertility of immigrants who had entered the United States as youths (under 12 years) was lower than that of any other life-cycle group

Table 3.11. Standardized Fertility Ratio, Foreign-Born, by Length of Residence in the United States, Erie County, 1900, 1915

1900		
Length of Residence	(N)	Fertility Ratio
Under 5 years	(181)	900
5–9 years	(262)	1,208
10–14 years	(39)	1,329
15–19 years	(378)	1,156
20–24 years	(185)	940
25 years or more	(405)	830
1915		
Length of Residence	(N)	Fertility Ratio
Under 5 years	(181)	926
5–9 years	(325)	1,087
10–14 years	(372)	1,214
15–19 years	(176)	1,070
20–24 years	(260)	957
25–29 years	(273)	906
30–34 years	(222)	681
35–39 years	(74)	531
40 years or more	(82)	361

Source: Calculated from New York State Census manuscripts.

Table 3.12. Standardized Fertility Ratio, by Migration and Marital Status, Foreign-Born, Erie County, 1915

Age at Migration	(N)	Fertility Ratio
Less than 12 years old	(391)	776
12–18 years old	(360)	892
19–24 years old	(564)	1,001
25 and over, single	(311)	971
25 and over, married	(301)	1,230

Source: Calculated from New York State Census manuscripts.

(776 per thousand). By contrast, the average fertility for those who had migrated as married adults was 1,230 per thousand (Table 3.12).

The impact of migration was not the same for every ethnic group. In 1915, the fertility of recent migrants, regardless of ethnicity, was similar, but that of long-time residents was quite distinctive. Poles, Italians, and Russians who had been in the county 10 to 14 years had fertility ratios of 1,499, 1,531, and 1,436 per thousand, respectively. Among those migrants who had been in the United States 25 to 29 years, fertility ranged from the Poles' 1,230 to the Russians' 683 per thousand (Table 3.13).

The Russian pattern was important. On average, for each year in the United States, Russian fertility fell 24.8 per thousand, nearly twice the rate of decline of any other group. Part of this decline may have been compositional—the overrepresentation of skilled workers among early immigrants. Still, the Russians appear to have adopted lower fertility more rapidly than other groups.

Life-cycle stage and occupation, too, were strongly related (Table 3.14). There was a marked difference in the relationship of fertility to occupation among those who migrated as children and as adults. Those who came as children or youths had occupational differentials that were similar to the native population—business class fertility was lower than working class fertility and inter-stratum differences between the old and new business class and skilled and unskilled workers were evident.

This pattern did not hold for those who had migrated when they were older. Working class fertility was actually lower than that of the business class for those who migrated as single adults, while among those who came as married adults, no pattern was obvious.

The relationship of migration to fertility had become more complex in the early twentieth century. Migration was now deeply etched in the opportunity structure. It no longer had the same impact on all ethnic and occupational groups. Those groups with greater access to the new opportunities—the skilled from Russia, those who had come when they were young—adopted low fertility rapidly, while those with less access did not.

The increasingly segmented labor market of the early twentieth century literally isolated many of the new immigrants from the new society. Those families cut off from the mainstream opportunity structure—either because of language, manners, or contacts—stayed behind the walls of their ethnic group. Coming to this country with an inferior labor market position and without much opportunity to rise in the social structure, they retained older patterns, including high fertility.

Indeed, for many of them America was not a new home, but a brief work site. The large share of the southern and eastern Europeans who migrated to America in the early twentieth century returned to their homeland. Between 1908 and 1923, two-thirds of the Romanians and Hungarians, 56 percent of the Southern Italians, and 40 percent of the Poles who migrated to the United States returned to Europe.[44]

Table 3.13. Standardized Fertility Ratio, by Length of Residence in U.S. and Birthplace, Foreign-Born, Erie County, 1915

Length of Residence	(N)	Birthplace					
		Canada	Germany	Austria-Hungary	Poland	Italy	Russia
Under 5 Years	(181)	269	765	681	935	1,486	798
5–9 years	(325)	923	947	958	1,180	1,325	1,127
10–14 years	(372)	660	924	1,231	1,499	1,531	1,436
15–19 years	(176)	631	904	1,011	1,150	1,305	733
20–24 years	(260)	551	854	1,112	1,213	1,344	864
25–29 years	(273)	428	941	986	1,230	1,071	683
30–34 years	(222)	481	623	547	1,086	1,110	129
35–39 years	(74)	254	335	—	521	—	—
40 years or more	(83)	136	335	—	176	—	—
Annual Decline of Ferility Ratio		10.3	13.7	3.3	9.8	13.0	24.8

SOURCE: Calculated from New York State Census manuscripts.
NOTE: Annual Decline = average decline in fertility per year in the United States.

Table 3.14. Standardized Fertility Ratio, Age at Migration and Occupation, Foreign-Born, Erie County, 1915

Occupational Stratum	Under 12	12–18	19–24	25 and over	
				Single	Married
N	(391)	(360)	(564)	(311)	(301)
Old business	698	800	808	1,214	1,142
New business	667	340	843	1,360	1,223
All workers	842	1,005	1,088	931	1,243
Skilled	817	919	1,016	923	1,108
Laborers	1,043	1,017	1,255	1,173	1,406

SOURCE: Calculated from New York State Census manuscripts.

"America for such workers," Gabriel Kolko notes, "was always a tentative, transitional experience, and protracted exposure to it did not make it more enduring." Their strategy was to limit expenses and save as much money as possible, hoping to return to their homeland and become well-off peasants. Rather than consider sending their children to school or adopting a higher standard of living, they "hoarded amazingly large proportions of their earnings even as they served in the lowest-skilled occupations."[45]

This reality—the melding of ethnic intentions and structural imperatives—explains in part the new immigrants' distinctive fertility pattern. The Russian Jews, who remained, moved quickly to lower their fertility, while the Italians, Poles, and those from Austria-Hungary—who left or intended to leave—did not. Those immigrants who had come as children or youths—really part of the second generation—adopted the fertility patterns of the native population, while those who came as adults had high fertility, whatever their occupation.

The interaction of culture and the segmentation of the labor market in the early twentieth century also segmented family strategies. At mid-century, the openness of the opportunity structure and its lack of correlation with transiency encouraged the individuation of migrants' family strategy. By 1900, migration and opportunity were negatively correlated. Newcomers tended to be temporary workers, cut off from or uninterested in opportunities for stability, and resistent to cultural change.

Those immigrants who had access to the primary working-class stratum, either because they came as skilled workers (like those from Russia) or because they had been raised in this country, moved to new patterns. The bulk of the new immigrants, however, remained isolated from the new culture. Their initial intentions—to remain peasants, earn money quickly, and return to Europe—were reinforced by common group experience. Rather than freeing them from traditional social control, their group experience reinforced the pillars of the old family regime and kept fertility high.

Conclusion

Fertility patterns in Erie County were incredibly complex. While the broad strokes of the fertility transition are clear, the closer one examines them, the more puzzling they become. The trick for the historian is to identify the general pattern without losing track of the exceptions.

Fertility declined rapidly between 1855 and 1915. The business class—especially professionals and business employees—limited family size sooner than workers, and skilled workers did so before the unskilled. Natives had lower fertility than the old immigrants, and the old immigrants had lower fertility than new immigrants. For the most part, these factors acted independently of one another: occupational differentials existed in all ethnic groups, and ethnic differentials in occupational groups.

At the risk of overstatement, we may conclude that the process of fertility decline was not evolutionary but revolutionary. While some strategies for restricting marital fertility through child spacing were evident, in general the movement to reduce fertility was closely related to the age pattern of family limitation. As Knodel and van de Walle have argued, family limitation was a new phenomenon, representing a decisive shift in *mentalité*.

The broad explanation of these trends and differentials lies in the changing family economies and class structure of nineteenth- and early twentieth-century society. Shifts in opportunities altered the logic of family formation and child rearing. For the business class, concerns over mobility and social status motivated families to have fewer children, send them to school, and raise standards of living. For the working class, the opening of clerical work and the decline of poverty encouraged skilled workers to consider new family strategies.

Yet this neat explanation of fertility decline was spoiled by the strength and resiliency of ethnic culture. The children of immigrants were more open to declining fertility than their parents, those who intermarried more than those who were endogamous, and early migrants more than later ones.

The segmentation of the labor force and the immigrants' short-term intentions cut them off from influences which led to lower fertility. The most stable group—those from Russia—and those who came to the United States as youths resembled the rest of the American population, but the bulk of the new immigrants retained a distinctive pattern. Adult migrants, who came ready to work for a few years and return to their peasant communities, gave the new immigrants their unique pattern.

This sea of data poses many questions about the process of social and cultural change, only a few of which we have answered. We have, to be honest, skirted one significant issue. So far, we have argued that the new immigrants' fertility resulted from the combination of structural conditions and cultural intentions. But which was it? Did the new immigrants— immersed in their peasant outlook—actively resist "the promise of American life"? Or did they take a hard look at social realities and decide that, for the time being, the old family strategy made more sense? Under what conditions and when did they decide to give the new social order a chance?

We can choose between the images of backward-looking primitive and hard-headed realist if we put the fertility choices of the immigrants in a wider perspective. Specifically, we can ask if the new immigrants rejected all social change or if they were selective, picking some and rejecting others. Therefore, in the next chapter, we examine education and fertility.

4

Schooling and Fertility in Erie County

EDUCATION is the Grand Central Station of the fertility decline. It was through education that parents hoped their children could take advantage of the new occupational opportunities. School attendance increased the cost of children and prolonged their dependency. Education opened the family to a wider range of cultural influences. However one explains the decline of fertility, it has to go by way of schooling.

The fact that education and fertility are related is hardly a novel insight. Proponents of the economic theory of fertility and the demographic transition have viewed increased schooling as an important correlate of fertility. According to the human-capital economists, the rise in the marginal cost of "child-production" resulted from the increased "inputs" required. Prolonged schooling and delayed labor-force entry were the decisive elements in the changing "investment strategy" of rational actors.

As we have seen, critics have attacked the economists for slighting cultural influences, using unmeasurable variables, and proposing untestable theoretical models. The economics of fertility "attempts to invalidate well-known sociological determinants of reproductive motivation," according to anthropologist Judith Blake. It "thus ends up with a framework to explain nonexistent facts, while [it] ignores or attempts to expunge explanations for existing ones."[1]

The new theorists of the demographic transition also consider education important. Caldwell's theory of fertility decline is based on the changing generational flow of wealth. In precapitalist peasant societies, the "familial mode of production" rests on the male's exploitation of women and children. With the breakdown of this system, women and children consume more and produce less. This change of direction in the net flow of wealth triggers the fertility transition.

Yet, for Caldwell, the change is far from automatic. The social and cultural props of the old system remain even after its economic operations are destroyed. Particularly during the early phases of change, the household head is able to insulate the family from these new circumstances. "Services within the house were provided on a subsistence basis by a familial mode of production not very different from that found in the peasant household." This two-tiered system—capitalist economy and pre-capitalist family—supported high fertility until the traditional family morality and culture were more fully undermined.[2]

Mass education dissolved this traditional culture. While Caldwell acknowledges the economic impact of education in decreased child labor and increased consumption, its cultural influence was most salient. Education identified the child as a future, not a present, worker; this imposed "middle-class" values; finally, education stressed universal values, not the particularistic ones of the family.[3]

Caldwell's theory is primarily concerned with social patterns at the beginning of the transition. As we noted in Chapter One, he is forced to admit that education influenced "different economic-demographic calculuses employed in the various social classes" after the fertility transition was under way. Furthermore, his theory has difficulties explaining why the upper-class parents were able to send their children to school for years without having their authority undercut or their fertility reduced.[4] Caldwell's difficulties in explaining group differentials is characteristic of the work of most demographers. Their neglect of nominal-level data and subpopulation variation has made it impossible for them to come to grips with the intricacies of the fertility transition.

Caldwell's portrayal of parents is unflattering. Jealously guarding their privilege, wary of the economic reality in which they live, parents give up their children to the state's new school system unwillingly. The school people, by contrast, are heroic; they liberate the children from the superstition and exploitation of their parents.[5]

Caldwell is a better demographer than he is an educational historian. He is quick to pass out the white and black hats in the education drama. But a more detailed investigation of the history of school attendance throws into question the neat story line that he wants to follow.

Caldwell's argument highlights the difficulty in disentangling the influence of social structure and of culture on family behavior. Particularly in the case of the new immigrant groups, many scholars have argued that cultural norms, not structural forces, motivated people's work and educational choices.

Virginia Yans-McLaughlin, for example, in her study of Italians in Buffalo, argued that the traditional "familistic" values of the Italian family affected women's work more than social or demographic realities. Since Yans-McLaughlin's focus on work is the flip side of our concern with education, and because she has studied the same city, her work provides an excellent test case for the interaction of society and culture.[6]

In this chapter, we will use detailed nominal-level data on adolescent schooling between 1850 and 1915 to study its impact on the fertility decline in Erie County. We cannot provide a direct test of Caldwell's theory, since mass education had already become common. Rather our concern is with the expansion of schooling among teenagers and the rise of mass high-school attendance.

Like the economists, in this analysis we will focus on the possible cost/benefit calculus of the families of Erie County. At the same time, following Caldwell, we will be concerned with the social and cultural changes that informed these choices. Particularly among immigrants, group experience was as important as indifference curves.

We have no direct evidence on parental exploitation of children. But our data do allow us an indirect test of parental attitudes toward increased schooling. If Caldwell were right, we would expect immigrants to resist further schooling until they were compelled by the authorities. Furthermore, if education had a generational impact, we would expect there to be a significant lag between the extension of schooling and the decline of fertility.

If, however, immigrants were well-meaning realists in an unequal society, we should find a different pattern. Parents would send their children to school voluntarily when they judged it in the children's interest. We would also expect decline in fertility and rise in education to be simultaneous, as parents moved quickly to take advantage of the new social context.

The evidence from Erie County suggests that unschooled parents kept their children in school. Innovation and emancipation did not flow only from the school to the working-class family. We cannot focus simply on the salubrious effect of education on nasty working-class parents; the families of Erie County moved quickly and voluntarily to give their children an edge in a changing and uncertain labor market.

One of the reasons Caldwell runs into trouble is his quick gloss on the history of education. In America, at least, recent work on the expansion of public schooling throws into doubt the traditional story.

The Working Class and American Educational History

American historians have been increasingly interested in education. A number of important issues—the character of class relations, the extent of social mobility, and the nature of reform movements—have centered on the character of the education system. Thus, when and why working-class children entered and stayed in public schools is now a crucial issue in American social history.

Traditionally, education and the working class was not a problematic field. The orthodox interpretation of American education—from Elwood Cubberley to Lawrence Cremin—presented the expansion of the school system as a response to the demands of working people for improved economic opportunity and training in democratic values.[7]

The expansion of elementary education in the mid-nineteenth century and the extension of secondary schooling during the Progressive period were, in this view, testimony to the robustness of the American tradition of reform from Jackson to Roosevelt. Whether they stressed consensus—the fundamental agreement on principles among all factions— or conflict—the workingman wresting his birthright from the forces of privilege and aristocracy—traditional educational historians told a story that confirmed Americans' belief in progress and the equity of the social order.

This was a good story, but bad history. Beginning with Michael Katz's *The Irony of Early School Reform* in 1967, a new generation of revisionist scholars broke with the traditional view. While the Progressive tradition had seen education as a prize the working class had won in battle, for the revisionists education was a means through which the well-off consolidated their power in American society. "The dominant theme in the twentieth century," according to Katz, "has been the attempt to adapt existing power relations to the development of a corporate industrial society."[8]

Recently, the revisionists themselves have come under attack. They have been accused of slandering the motives of educational reformers and ignoring the positive effects of schooling. The revisionists have countered that their case rests on the existence neither of a Machiavellian ruling class nor a permanently degraded working class. Calling for "more sophisticated models of class and class relations," Katz has argued that the "popular acceptance of public education represented ideological hegemony." While schooling was "imposed" on the working class, this does not "imply conspiracy or malevolence." Rather, the support of schooling represented "the unselfconscious and willing acceptance of a direction imposed on social life by the dominant fundamental group."[9]

The debate between the revisionists and their critics has focused scholars' attention on the actual behavior of working people and the gap between official intent and popular action. David Hogan found that education was one variable in the complex calculus of working-class survival. "In effect, immigrant parents experienced a tension between survival and schooling," notes Hogan. "The exigencies of economic survival in a wage labor society created . . . a conflict between making a sufficient living in order for their children to go to school and the necessity to go to school in order to make an adequate living."[10]

Economic and social forces, however, were overlaid with cultural concerns, particularly the immigrants' suspicion of the "Americanizing" function of public schools. While groups varied in their assessment of the impact of schooling, they all accepted the logic of increased school: "their beliefs about the economic significance of education . . . proved to be crucial in determining their educational behavior."[11]

Miriam Cohen's study of Italian and Jewish families in New York City during the early twentieth century has also focused on the impact of family economy and strategy on work and education. According to Cohen, schooling and work were less affected by cultural differences than by the socioeconomic condition of each group. She notes that

> historians have generally assumed that an increase in school attendance reflected aspects of behavioral and attitudinal changes that occurred as immigrants abandoned Old-World familial values and adopted American values, such as individualism, and American middle-class family styles, which emphasized the needs of children rather than those of adults.[12]

Yet, rather than representing a process of "embourgeoisement," the increase in ethnic school attendance was the result of "a shift in working class family strategies which were made necessary by the changes in the city's employment structure." While Jewish women attended school longer than Italian women at the turn of the century, Cohen attributes this to the Jewish parents' higher occupational status, not the Italians' cultural bias. Indeed, with the expansion of the city's clerical sector during the 1920s and 1930s, Italian women actually stayed in school longer than Italian men. The changing value of public education, not cultural sexism, explains the behavior of Italian parents.[13]

Hogan's and Cohen's arguments provide important conceptualizations of working class educational behavior. They are both limited, however, by their reliance on published aggregate data. Joel Perlmann's study of Providence, Rhode Island, on the other hand, uses a large nominal-level data base to study schooling around the turn of the century.[14]

Perlmann argues that high-school attendance rates among social classes became "more equal" between 1880 and 1925. Yet the differences between occupational strata remained significant. Over a third of white-collar workers' sons attended high school in 1900, but this figure rose to 53 percent in 1915 and then to 71 percent in 1925. The attendance of skilled workers also rose substantially, from 13 percent in 1900 to 53 percent in 1925, while unskilled workers went from a rate of only 12 percent in 1915 to 30 percent in 1925.[15]

Although Perlmann is technically correct that high-school attendance became more equal over the period, this fact is simply an outcome of the high proportion of white-collar children already in high school in 1880. While the two-and-a-half-fold increase in the skilled workers' rate is impressive, we must remember that even if all white-collar workers' children were in high school by 1925, this would not have increased their rate of school attendance as quickly as skilled workers. Indeed, if post-secondary education were considered, it is doubtful that total educational achievement did become more equal. The equalization that Perlmann finds is a product of what he examines and how he chooses to measure it.[16]

The more interesting aspect of Perlmann's work is the timing of the increase in high-school attendance. Before 1900, high school was almost entirely an experience for white-collar children, but in the years that followed, blue-collar children's attendance increased quite rapidly. In spite of this upsurge, however, the difference between high-school attendance by the children of skilled and of unskilled workers remained substantial throughout the first quarter of the century.

Following the lead of Hogan, Cohen, and Perlmann, this chapter will examine four questions. What were the trends in high school attendance in Erie County between 1850 and 1915? How can we explain the sexual, class, and ethnic differentials in school attendance? What forces in the economy and society were related to these differences in school attendance? Finally, what was the relationship of trends in education to the fertility transition?

The data for this chapter are both better and worse than what we have used earlier. Since the 1855 census did not include a question on school attendance, we have included data from the 1850, 1870, and 1880 Federal Censuses. Therefore we have data at five points between 1850 and 1915. On the other hand, in only one year, 1900, can we directly link fertility and education. For the nineteenth century, we have no fertility data, and for 1915, we can only link the two factors ecologically.

Our basic measure of school attendance is the percent of youths, ages 15–19, who attended school during the previous year. The age of 15 was chosen because during most of this period 15 was recognized as the decisive age for choosing whether to continue in school or not. For example, in 1850, 54 percent of the 14-year-old boys in our sample were in school, but only 30 percent of the 15-year-olds.[17]

School Attendance in Erie County

Between 1850 and 1915, school attendance among older teenagers in Erie County tripled. In 1850, only 12 percent of the boys and 13 percent of the girls between the ages of 15 and 19 had attended school during the previous year. By 1915, the rates were 37 percent for boys and for girls (Table 4.1).

This increase did not occur steadily. Rather, it coincided with the two great periods of school reform. During the school reform period at

Table 4.1. Percent of Children, Aged 15–19, Attending School, by Gender, Erie County, 1850–1915

Gender	1850	1870	Year 1880	1900	1915
Males	11.7%	20.6%	22.6%	23.7%	37.4%
Females	12.8	18.5	25.9	29.5	36.9

SOURCE: Calculated from U.S. and New York State Census manuscripts.

midcentury—when the public high school first emerged—school attendance jumped from 12 percent to 21 percent for boys and from less than 13 to more than 18 percent for girls. Then after a period of relative stability, school attendance again rose during the Progressive period (1900 to 1915), from 24 to 37 percent for boys and from 30 to 37 percent for girls.

Boys' and girls' rates of high-school attendance were never more than a few percentage points apart, except in 1900, when the girls' rate was nearly 16 percent greater than the boys'. This gap was largely the result of the different strategies that working class parents took toward educating the sexes.

The relationship between father's occupation and high-school attendance shifted throughout the period. In 1870, there was a difference in the boys' rate of school attendance—the business-class rate was 27 percent, and the working-class rate, 20 percent. Among girls, class differences ran in the opposite direction. The highest rate among the girls was the non-skilled workers' (22 percent), while only 10 percent of the daughters of the old business class attended school (Table 4.2).

By 1880, expected class differentials were more clear-cut. While the rates for all business-class groups except old business-class boys rose substantially, those among average working-class children declined. One in five sons of unskilled workers attended school in 1870, but a decade later their rate was 14 percent. The stability in school attendance between 1870 and 1880 was only apparent, a combination of increasing school attendance among the children of the business class and declining school attendance among the working class.

By 1900, the sexual and class divisions in high-school attendance had become clearer. While the boys' rate had advanced moderately for old business-class families (30 percent), school attendance exploded among the new business class (69 percent). By contrast, there was no change for working-class boys.

Class differentials increased among girls between 1880 and 1900. The range between the highest and lowest rate doubled from 12 percentage points to 24 percentage points. The new and old business class rates increased to 56 and 37 percent, respectively. While the non-skilled rate remained the same (22 percent), the rate for the daughters of skilled workers jumped to 29 percent.

During the first fifteen years of this century, the demography of the high-school population changed quickly. The old business class finally

Table 4.2.   Percent of Children, Aged 15–19, Attending School, by Father's Occupational Category and Stratum, Erie County, 1870–1915

	Males				Females			
Father's Occupational Category	1870	1880	1900	1915	1870	1880	1900	1915
Professionals	NA	66.7%	85.6%	76.7%	NA	30.7%	45.5%	50.6%
Agents and Merchants	NA	30.4	15.3	50.4	NA	32.1	34.4	42.6
Service and Semi-professional	NA	20.0	30.2	41.6	NA	28.6	36.5	43.6
Business Employees	NA	33.3	53.1	52.2	NA	30.0	61.0	56.1
Government Employees	NA	0.0	43.2	45.6	NA	38.5	51.1	42.1
Masters and Manufacturers	NA	28.6	44.4	39.8	NA	6.7	34.3	36.5
Skilled Workers	NA	21.7	21.0	32.1	NA	17.9	29.0	28.4
Transport Workers	NA	23.5	15.0	34.8	NA	25.0	25.2	28.4
Other Workers	NA	13.0	13.5	28.4	NA	38.9	29.5	31.8
Laborers	NA	12.2	13.2	22.6	NA	16.7	19.4	21.7
Father's Occupational Stratum								
Old Business	27.2%	25.0	30.5	45.9	9.5%	27.3	37.2	50.2
New Business	26.7	44.4	68.9	55.3	17.1	30.4	55.9	57.9
Skilled Workers	19.7	21.7	21.0	32.1	17.2	17.9	29.0	28.4
Non-skilled Workers	20.3	13.9	14.1	28.2	22.1	21.8	21.8	26.6
Agricultural Workers	NA	42.9	26.2	22.3	NA	47.3	39.9	34.2

SOURCE: Calculated from U.S. and New York State Census manuscripts.

began to keep its children in school almost as long as the new business class; the differentials among boys (9 percentage points) and girls (8 percentage points) were sharply lower than those in previous years.

The most important variation, however, was among working-class boys. While the girls' rates held steady (skilled declined less than 1 percentage point, non-skilled increased by 5 percentage points), the attendance rates for sons of skilled workers rose by over half, to 32 percent. More notably, the non-skilled rate doubled from 14 to 28 percent.

While the general contours of Erie County high-school attendance were similar to those found by Perlmann in Providence, the attendance rates of non-skilled children were different in the two cities. In Providence, the differential between skilled and unskilled workers remained sharp, while in Erie County it declined between 1900 and 1915.

To some extent this difference is statistical. The differential between the sons of skilled workers and laborers remained quite large in 1915 (32 to 23 percent), although not as large as that in Providence. Recall as well, Perlmann's data were based on enrollment in secondary school while the present figures are for all schooling. It could be that many immigrant children were held back in elementary school. These children would show up in our data, but not in Perlmann's.

The relationship of high-school attendance to precise occupational categories is largely consistent with the trends among strata. Among the six business-class groups, professionals and business employees consistently had the highest rates for boys. The most dramatic change occurred among merchants and agents. In 1900, less than one in six boys in this group had attended school; by 1915 this figure was one in two. The rate among sons of service and semi-professionals also increased sharply, from 20 percent in 1880 to 42 percent in 1915.

By 1915, the diversity of the business class had disappeared. Secondary schooling had become a class experience. As late as 1900, the range in rates among boys of fathers in business-class occupations had been 70 percentage points; by 1915 it had been reduced to 37 percentage points.[18]

The difference in the high-school attendance rates of boys and girls raises some troubling questions about the role of education in early twentieth-century Erie County. Although for the population as a whole there was little gender difference in the rates, the class differentials among boys were sharper than those among the girls. In 1870, working-class girls attended school more often than business-class girls, while the gap among boys was quite large, in favor of the business stratum. These differentials changed over time, but the gaps between the boys' rate were consistently more related to class than were the girls'.

Male high-school attendance rates were more sensitive to changes in the labor market than were female rates. During the nineteenth century, as Katz and Davey have noted, the high-school curriculum was directed at a white-collar constituency. For the working class of Hamilton, Ontario, it was little more than a refuge from a slack labor market. In Hamilton, the improvement of the economy between 1861 and 1871 actually led to a decrease in working-class school attendance.[19]

During the early twentieth century, however, working-class children streamed into high schools. On the one hand, youths were pushed out of the labor market by technology and protective legislation. At the same time, the Progressive education movement gave birth to the "child-centered" school and vocationalism, which pulled in more working-class youths. Finally, the changes in the working-class standard of living that we examined in Chapter Two allowed greater possibility of prolonged education.[20]

These forces did not affect the entire working class. The split between its primary and secondary sector was clearly related to standard of living and fertility. As these data make clear, it also was reinforced by high-school attendance. The skilled workers of the primary sector increasingly kept their sons in school; parents in the secondary sector—while prolonging their sons' schooling—still sent a large proportion of them into the labor force.

These social structural forces were muted for women. Working-class parents shared the business-class assumption that women would work only until they married. Female high-school attendance was less closely related to work and more tied to the immediate needs of the family and to cultural norms. Only the rise of the clerical job market late in the nineteenth century more closely wed female school attendance to labor-market realities.

While the reform of the labor market was an important element of Progressive education, it had a cultural dimension as well: Americanization. Progressives hoped that educational reform would assimilate millions of immigrants and their children to American culture and democratic values.

If simple rates of high-school attendance are a measure, this movement was a success. By the end of our study, immigrants were sending their children to high school in greater and greater numbers.

The sons of native-born Americans went to school longer than those of foreign-born parents (Table 4.3). In 1870, one-third of the sons of natives were attending high school, while no foreign-born group sent more than a fifth of its sons to school. In 1880 and 1900, our data allow us to judge the differences between native-born of native and foreign parentage, differences that also were substantial. For example, in 1900, attendance rates for natives of native parentage were 44 percent for boys and 51 percent for girls, while native-born of foreign parentage sent their children to school less often, but still at rates higher than immigrants. The rate for sons of natives of Irish parentage was 40 percent compared with 33 percent for the sons of the Irish-born. For Germans, the rates were 20 percent for grandsons and 14 percent for sons of German-born parents.

The biggest surprise among immigrants in 1900 was the Germans. While the high-school attendance rates of the sons of Canadian and Irish fathers were 25 and 33 percent, the rate for the sons of Germans was a mere 14 percent. Only the newly arrived Poles sent their sons to school proportionally less (8 percent).

The Germans continued to have a low high-school attendance among their sons in 1915. The native, Irish, English, and Canadian rates continued to be above that of the Germans. Furthermore, all of the new immigrants groups—from Poland, Italy, Russia, and Austria-Hungary—had rates higher than the Germans, in spite of the recency of their migration and their poverty.

The low high-school attendance rates of Germans is a curiosity. In 1855, the Germans were better off than the other major ethnic group, the Irish. In addition to higher economic standing, the Germans were concentrated in skilled jobs, while the Irish were predominantly unskilled. But the Germans were less quick to move into the business class, remaining skilled workers instead, although hardly to be compared to the less skilled new immigrants.[21] (See Table 2.4.)

Structural and cultural forces played a part in explaining the Germans' low attendance rates. Labor recruitment in the early twentieth century had not yet passed to centralized employment offices. Rather, foremen and skilled workers had significant control over the hiring of their workers well into the twentieth century.[22]

This situation benefited youths of German background. Since their fathers controlled so many of the city's skilled jobs, they always had ready access to the skilled job market. While other immigrants relied on formal

Table 4.3. Percent of Children, Aged 15–19, Attending School, by Parents' Birthplace and Ethnicity, Erie County, 1870–1915

Parents' Birthplace	Males				Females			
	1870	1880	1900	1915	1870	1880	1900	1915
Native-born	33.3%	NA	NA	42.7%	18.4%	NA	NA	40.8%
Native father	NA	42.3%	44.4%	NA	NA	50.0%	50.6%	NA
Irish father	NA	26.2	39.5	NA	NA	29.0	47.1	NA
German father	NA	12.5	20.3	NA	NA	11.2	25.5	NA
Other father	NA	11.8	32.9	NA	NA	25.7	30.9	NA
Canada	8.7	25.0	24.7	49.8	30.8	28.6	45.1	44.5
Ireland	17.9	0.0	32.8	35.5	18.6	0.0	56.4	41.8
Germany	13.8	3.2	14.5	19.5	14.8	13.8	14.7	21.0
England	19.5	NA	NA	38.2	19.5	NA	NA	36.4
Poland	NA	NA	7.5	25.4	NA	NA	8.0	13.1
Austria-Hungary	NA	NA	NA	30.4	NA	NA	NA	13.1
Italy	NA	NA	NA	35.2	NA	NA	NA	28.9
Russia	NA	NA	NA	47.3				40.8

SOURCE: Calculated from U.S. and New York State Census manuscripts.

education to make it in America, the Germans could use their direct connections to the labor market to ignore secondary education. Even German girls, who did not benefit from the skilled labor market, avoided high-school.

Culture, too, kept Germans out of the high schools. While many of them were Catholics, the parochial education system, like the Church in general, was controlled by Irish Catholics. Therefore, unlike the Irish who could avoid the suspected nativism of the public schools by forming an extensive parochial system, the Germans did not have high schools of their own.[23]

As always, it is difficult to disentangle the structural and cultural elements of the Germans' behavior. Yet even compared to other non-Irish Catholic groups—the Italians and Poles—the Germans had still lower attendance rates. Their control of the skilled job market, rather than their cultural situation, was probably more important in explaining their low rate of school attendance.

The most notable feature of the ethnic patterns in 1915 was the clear gender differences among newer immigrant groups. For the most part, when a gender differential was significant, it favored girls. But in 1915, male attendance rates of all newer immigrant groups were substantially higher than for females. The smallest gender differential was among those of parents born in Russia (47 percent of sons and 41 percent of daughters) and in Italy (35 and 29 percent), while the gap between male and female rates for the Poles (25 and 13 percent) and Austro-Hungarians (30 and 13 percent) was substantial.

These results, again, raise the question about the roles of culture and of social structure in determining school attendance. Cohen, as we noted, contends that the history of female school attendance is the result of changing labor market conditions; working-class women rapidly entered the labor market when opportunities opened. Yans-McLaughlin, in her study of Italians in Buffalo, contends that the distinctive gender differences in education of the children of immigrants demonstrate the continued strength of immigrant culture.

According to Yans-McLaughlin the distinctive features of Italian immigrants—their low occupational status and school attendance—was a product of the cultural values of "familism and male superiority." She argues that "there was a lot of room in some late nineteenth and early twentieth century cities for immigrant families who wished to avoid a head-on collision with the new way of life." Cultural preferences as well as social structure played a role in shaping patterns of work and schooling. Thus "traditional family values acted as an independent variable, and the occupational opportunities of industrial cities provided enough variation for individual families to find work arrangements appropriate for their cultural needs."[24]

Structure and culture interacted in complex ways. An interpretation that ignores either is unconvincing. In response to the criticism of Tilly and Cohen, Yans-McLaughlin suggested that we need a perspective which reflects "ethnic and cultural variations" by employing a "highly eclectic methodology capable of defining such objective conditions as economic, demographic, and occupational structure, and changes in these structures over time."[25]

The evidence from Erie County qualifies Yans-McLaughlin's cultural argument. While it is true that Italians were distinctive in their avoidance of factory labor for men and domestic service for women, their high school attendance pattern was hardly unique. Rather than following tradition—keeping their daughters at home away from outside influences—they sent them to high school. Compared to the other new immigrants, their rate of female high-school attendance was high and the gap between male and female rates was low.

While Yans-McLaughlin is correct in stressing the independence of culture and society, these data suggest that the balance must be much closer to the structural pole than she would have it. For Yans-McLaughlin, changes in the labor force and educational behavior take place within the confines of immigrant culture.

We might picture culture as a box (or in Yans-McLaughlin's phrase, "new wine in old bottles") which allows for some movement, but which sets limits on how much variation is possible. Yet the data on school attendance suggest that cultural boundaries were easily crossed.

Rather than a box, sturdy and confining, immigrant culture may have been less rigid. It provided some constraints on behavior, but as structural forces became stronger, it gave way altogether. As long as the structural forces were not too strong, cultural norms held sway, but only to a point. Ultimately, they were overwhelmed by the demands of the labor market; at that point the immigrants formulated a new strategy more consistent with new realities.

This may explain the gender differences in high-school attendance. The economic opportunities of women in the early twentieth century were so few that education was of limited use. Ethnic groups could retain their "traditional" patterns in this situation. Natives and old immigrants sent their daughters to school; Italians could combine school and work at home; and Poles could send their daughters off to the box factory.

For boys, the cultural norms broke down more quickly. The new opportunities for white-collar jobs and vocational education swept away old constraints. All boys—Poles and Jews, Italians and Hungarians—stayed in school longer than their sisters.

These data, then, allow us to sort out some of the complexities in the relationship of culture to social change. The culture of the new immigrants provided a set of goals and expectations that were at variance with the realities of American society. Families employed two strategies to deal with this gap between expectations and claims: they could cushion themselves from the main society or they could change their expectations to be more consistent with the conditions they faced.

High-school attendance suggests that they were able to cushion themselves to some extent. Girls—still defined as non-workers by both natives and immigrants—attended high school less often than boys, and this pattern was more related to culture than occupation or class. For boys, the workers of the future, cultural norms had little influence on schooling. The economic needs of the family and the realities of the labor market determined who went to school and how long they stayed.[26]

Social class, ethnicity, and the job market were the key influences on school attendance in Erie County. Changes in the labor market increased the attractiveness of schooling for both the business and working classes. At the same time, the two explosions in school attendance corresponded with the two educational reform movements: the 1850s and the early twentieth century.

In spite of the rise in school attendance for the population as a whole, the class character of schooling in Erie County became more clearly etched between 1870 and 1915. At the turn of the century, business-class youths were two or three times as likely to be attending school as the children of the working class. By 1915, a greater proportion of working-class children were in school, but the differentials remained strong.

Ethnic differences both complemented and complicated these patterns. Most groups increased school attendance; only the Germans resisted the trend. At the same time, the gender differences among newer immigrants suggest that older cultural norms had a significant, if delimited and perhaps declining, role in determining family strategies in the industrial city.

Fertility and Education

The same social, economic, and cultural forces influenced the prolongation of school attendance and the decline of fertility in Erie County. On the one hand, the restructuring of the labor market and class relations, the opening of the opportunity structure, and rising standards of living encouraged the logic of fewer, better-educated children. On the other hand, cultural norms concerning the goals of family life and proper roles channeled and qualified the transition to a smaller family.

The data from Erie County, however, do not support the contention that the move to prolong education was resisted by tradition-bound parents. While some immigrant groups were less willing to send their children to school, the bulk of evidence suggests that when schooling became an important and meaningful strategy for success, most segments of the population moved quickly to take advantage of it.[27]

In this section we need to examine the second corollary of Caldwell's thesis: that there was a substantial lag between the rise of schooling and the decline of fertility. If the impact of education on fertility had been primarily to "rationalize" working-class behavior—as modernization theorists would have it—we would expect a generation gap between the rise of schooling and the decline of fertility. Only as the "modern" products of the educational system became parents would fertility begin to fall.

The economists, too, have an image of the relationship of fertility to education. As individual couples evaluated the costs/benefits of low fertility and prolonged schooling in the context of their tastes and of market constraints, economists would predict a slow and steady decline in fertility and a rise in school attendance as the wages of families slowly improved. Fertility decline and educational expansion would be a slow, evolutionary process.

Neither of these expectations—generational lag nor evolutionary change—were met. The decline of fertility was sudden and simultaneous with the extension of schooling. After a period of forty-five years in which the fertility of skilled workers had declined at a rate of less than one-half of one percent, in the first fifteen years of this century the rate of decline more than tripled.

The decline of fertility was neither a simple quantitative change nor a diffusion of a new set of attitudes. It was a qualitative change in the family strategy of the working class. Education and fertility were elements of the same phenomenon.

While the data suggest that the two events—declining fertility and extension of education—happened at the same time and can be explained with similar arguments, we do not know if these two variables were directly related. This question raises a methodological problem. Since women with children of high-school age are at least in their thirties, we cannot use the current fertility estimates on which we have relied.

We use two strategies to get around this problem. First, we look at the aggregate relationship of the two variables to determine if they were related at the group level (occupation and ethnicity). Second, we use the children-ever-born data from 1900 to examine the direct relationship between them at the individual level.

On an aggregate level, high-school attendance and fertility were connected in 1900 and 1915. The new business class had both the lowest fertility and highest school attendance in both years. The old business class, skilled workers, and non-skilled workers all followed in the same rank order for both fertility and school attendance.

The ranking of ethnic groups was also similar for both variables. Natives and children of Canadians had the lowest fertility and highest school attendance, while the newer immigrant groups were at the opposite end of both scales. Two ethnic groups did not fit the pattern. The children of German descent had unexpectedly low school attendance given their fertility. The children of the Russian-born, on the other hand, had the expected high fertility of a new immigrant group (although lower than the Poles and Italians), but had the second highest school attendance rate.

The 1900 children-ever-born data allow us to examine this relationship at the nominal level, but they too have drawbacks. While 1900 was a pivotal year in the history of education and fertility, it was prior to the immense change in working-class behavior. Still, it provides some insight into the decision making of individual families.[28]

For the entire population, those families with all of their teenage children in school were much more likely to have small families than were those with none at school (Table 4.4). Those families with no boys at school had an estimated number of children ever born of 7.2, twenty-five percent higher than the figure for families with attenders. Among girls, non-attending families' fertility was 6.8 compared to 5.4 for attending families.[29]

But was education's influence on fertility independent of class and ethnicity? To answer this question we used multiple classification analysis

Table 4.4. Estimated Children-Ever-Born, By School Attendance of Children, Aged 15–19, in Household and Occupation, Multiple Classification Analysis, Erie County, New York, 1900

| Occupation and Childdren's School Attendance | Controlling for | | | |
| | age and age-at-marriage | | age, age-at-marriage, and ethnicity | |
	Males	Females	Males	Females
All Occupations				
No children at school	7.2	6.8	6.9	6.5
All children at school	5.7	5.4	6.2	5.8
Old Business Class				
No children at school	6.3	6.1	6.4	6.0
All children at school	5.0	4.7	5.6	5.3
New Business Class				
No children at school	6.2	5.4	6.5	5.4
All children at school	4.7	5.0	5.3	5.6
Skilled Workers				
No children at school	6.9	6.4	7.0	6.2
All children at school	6.4	5.3	6.3	5.5
Non-skilled Workers				
No children at school	7.8	7.5	7.3	6.8
All children at school	6.6	6.6	6.6	6.6

SOURCE: Calculated from U.S. Census manuscripts.

to control for the influence of social class, ethnicity, and woman's age at marriage. This substantially reduces the relationship between education and fertility; it is about half of the uncontrolled difference. Still, the influence of education, even if controlled, is statistically significant.[30]

Children's education was related to parents' fertility for all occupational strata. The fertility of business-class families with no male high-school students was approximately thirty percent higher than that for those with students. Among the working class families, the differences were smaller: 8 percent for boys among skilled workers and 17 percent for non-skilled workers.

The relationship of fertility to occupational stratum and daughter's high-school attendance was similar. The contrasts between families with attenders and with non-attenders were 28 percent and 8 percent for the business classes, and 22 and 13 percent for the working-class strata.

If we control these findings for ethnicity, however, the clarity of the female high-school attendance pattern by father's occupational stratum disappears. The fertility differentials between families with and without male high-school students remain large, ranging from 22 percent for the new business class to 10 percent for both working-class strata. But among families with women of high-school age, the differentials are greatly reduced; only for the old business and skilled worker strata are they substantial.

What do these data tell us about the impact of education on fertility? First, they point to the importance of *boys'* attendance as an index of family strategy. Girls were not seen as future workers who needed an education to succeed in life; thus, the decision to send a girl to school was governed more by cultural considerations or the individual needs of the family than by the "remaking" of working-class family strategies.[31]

Among boys, both their own education and their father's occupation had important independent influences on their mother's fertility. The differences within occupational strata remained important, as did those between social classes. Yet, the gap between the new and old business strata disappeared in the multivariate analysis, while that between skilled and nonskilled workers was greatly reduced.

Boys' high-school attendance, then, had two impacts on fertility in 1900. On the one hand, it represented part of the differing family strategies of the various social classes and strata. At the same time, within classes those families that led the movement to extended schooling were the same families that limited their fertility. The relationship of schooling and family size resulted from the combination of social structural and individual motivation.

We must end our analysis, however, with a note of caution. These 1900 data were too early for us to examine fully the transformation of working-class family strategies. The fertility data for this analysis concerned women who had had their children between 1870 and 1900, before the fertility transition had fully affected working-class families. At the same time, in 1900, high school remained a business-class phenomenon. A business-class youth was nearly twice as likely to be in school as was a working-class teenager. Buffalo and Erie County were poised at the beginning of the great transformation of the working-class family.

Conclusion

Working-class families used education to adapt to the exigencies of the labor market in the late nineteenth and early twentieth centuries. Schooling was clearly related to the ethnic and occupational structure of

Erie County. The same forces which influenced fertility—the rise in standards of living and increased opportunities for educated labor—led also to the increase in working-class high-school attendance.

This connection was not present simply at the group level. Even within social classes and ethnic groups, those families that sent their children—especially their boys—to high school were the same ones that lowered their fertility. The connection between the two was simultaneous and direct.

The transition was particularly striking among working-class families. In Erie County as in Providence, Rhode Island, skilled-worker children's high-school attendance exploded between 1900 and 1915 at the same time that their parents' fertility tumbled. These parents quickly adapted to the new set of circumstances and changed their family strategy to improve the lives of their children. The speed of these changes and their simultaneity suggest that neither the simple economic nor modernization theories can explain the difference.

Caldwell's image of working-class parents jealously guarding their power and hampering their children's futures does not jibe with the data from Erie County. When standards of living and the labor market changed in the late nineteenth century, working-class parents quickly changed their strategy to benefit their children. Education did not simply emancipate children from the exploitation of their parents.

Nor does a simple cost/benefit model work. The change in fertility was both an individual and a group process. Each family did not calculate its own equations and then make its own plan. The new family strategy was embedded in the group experience of the families of Erie County.

The decline in fertility can only be explained in the context of the structure of inequality that defined class relations in American society. Before the turn of the century, the spectre of poverty was a constant concern of the working-class family. Poverty defined the elements of its family strategy: boarding, child labor, and predictable deprivation.

Suddenly, in the years around the turn of the century, the situation changed. A quantitative improvement in the standard of living was transformed into a qualitative change in the possibilities of working-class life. A stratum of the working class could, for the first time, expect a life without poverty. What had been unthinkable became thinkable; the uncontrolled was now controllable.

This change was not simply the diffusion of middle-class norms. Despite the widespread adoption of low fertility and prolonged schooling, working class families resisted these changes throughout the last half of the nineteenth century. Only when the new patterns made sense in terms of their own lives did they change.

The history of schooling and fertility provides a glimpse as well into the process of cultural change and its relationship to social reality. The social forces gathered over a period of decades; as we saw in Chapter Two, incomes slowly increased, the opportunity structure opened incrementally.

But the impact of these forces on the cognitive world of the working class happened suddenly. Around the turn of the century, the working class "saw" the transformation of society around it and moved suddenly to take advantage of it. Social structure was "real" only when it changed the way that working-class parents saw the world in which they lived.

5

Rural Fertility in Erie County

The city was the focus of the American imagination in the late nineteenth century. Great fortunes were accumulated; technology and capital were combined to create the new factories and corporations; immigrant communities became the seedbeds for a new definition of American life. The nation's great metropolises—New York, Chicago, Philadelphia—were where history was being made.

The countryside did not take well to this. The Grange, the Alliance movement, and Populism were all implicit indictments of the emerging urban, industrial society. These movements, and right-wing Protestant fundamentalism, symbolized by the Scopes monkey trial, fixed the image of the country "yahoo"—backward-looking, intolerant, "anti-modern"— in American culture.[1]

But demographers had a surprise. It was the countryside, not the city, that was the source of the fertility decline. Beginning with Yasuba and continuing through the work of Easterlin and Vinovskis, demographic historians found that rural family size began to fall early in the nineteenth century and that the trend was well established by 1840. Who were these modern anti-modernists?[2]

Indeed, with few exceptions, the work of American researchers has been concerned with the contours of rural fertility. The land-availability thesis and the work of those who have attacked it have dominated American historical demography.

Scholars have focused on urban fertility more in the past decade. Inspired by European researchers or the painful theorizing of the Chicago economists, a host of historians have examined the trends and differentials of family size in cities across the nation. Much of the present study is a contribution to this literature.

For the most part the two topics—urban and rural fertility—have remained separate. The differentials between the two have been dutifully noted, and then researchers have burrowed away into their specific area. Little attempt has been made to extend the theories of rural fertility to the city, or vice versa.

This is the task of the present chapter. We have already sketched an analytical scheme for understanding the fertility transition and examined these trends in Erie County. While the data have been concerned with all of Erie County, we have focused for the most part on *urban* social structure.

Both the methods and concepts we have already used can be transferred to rural fertility. Our primary methodological concern—the use of nominal-level data to examine differentials within a geographical unit—is obviously relevant in a rural setting, although few studies have taken advantage of this kind of data.

The chief conceptual issue—the impact of social structural and cultural divisions within the population—might seem more problematic. The American countryside does not usually call up images of class and ethnic division. But just as we were surprised by the "modernity" of rural Americans' fertility, we may find that the image of a "classless" countryside is also misleading.

The only intensive study of the impact of social structure on rural fertility is Wendell Bash's study of fertility in Madison County, New York. Using the children-ever-born data from the New York State census of 1865, Bash was able to examine several dimensions of differential fertility.[3]

As in urban studies, Bash found that immigrant fertility was over fifty percent higher than native fertility. He also discovered clear occupational differences: white-collar groups had the lowest fertility, followed by skilled workers and farm proprietors. The highest fertility groups were tenant farmers and unskilled workers.

Economic standing—defined as dwelling value—was negatively correlated with fertility. Those with homes worth over $600 had a fertility rate a third lower than those with homes worth less than $300. Finally, those with the most and the least valuable farms had higher fertility than those on farms of middling value.

Given the sharp differences found by Bash, it is surprising that so little has been made of social structural influences on rural fertility. In spite of all the uproar over interstate differentials, Bash's work suggests that much of the variation in the fertility experience of rural families could be explained through an examination of their distribution in social, not geographical, space.

Erie County provides an excellent setting for examining the role of class and ethnicity on rural fertility. In sharp contrast to the city of Buffalo, the rest of the county was composed of agricultural areas and some sixteen villages of varying sizes that served as service centers and commercial entrepots.

Settlement began in most parts of Erie County during the first decade of the nineteenth century, and by 1855 considerable progress had been made in establishing a successful agricultural area. The region had two distinct types of farmland: the flat grain-growing area of the north and the hilly livestock-grazing area to the south. By midcentury, the county was a varied, dynamic region on its way to becoming one of the leading agricultural areas of the state.[4]

The spectacular growth of Buffalo should not obscure the economic health of rural Erie County. Between 1840 and 1855, as the population of Buffalo more than doubled—from 35,000 to 72,000—that of rural Erie County rose from 44,000 to 60,000.

In 1855, the average head of household had lived in Erie County for six years longer than his counterpart in Buffalo. Although the proportion who had lived in Buffalo for under five years was greater than in the county (44 to 36 percent), the share for less than one year was quite similar (16 to 14 percent). In spite of the pull of a dynamic city, rural Erie County remained an attractive residential location. Proximity to Buffalo and the Erie Canal provided the base for a vital, prosperous economy.

European immigrants were important to the county's development. While few Irish were farmers, German-born household heads composed a third of the agricultural population. Although more stable and native than the city, rural Erie County was representative of the rapid growth of American rural society before the Civil War.[5]

The Class Structure of Rural Erie County

Erie County grew quickly, but its prosperity was not distributed evenly. Ethnic divisions, rather, were reinforced by distinctions of wealth and status. Social class was a fact of life in the countryside, just as it was in the city.

Three social classes are possible in an agricultural setting: land-owners, farm workers, and tenant farmers. In their analysis of rural fertility, Easterlin, George Alter, and Gretchen Condran found that farm workers—the rural proletariat—were not a large or significant stratum of rural Amerian society in the mid-nineteenth century. But what of tenant farmers? Were they a significant element of the social structure?[6]

Historians have considered the problem of tenancy and absentee ownership of agricultural land the unique problem of the Southern United States. Many of the special elements of that region's experience—Jim Crow, radical Populism, and economic backwardness—have been associated with the predominance of tenancy and sharecropping. Like slavery, tenancy is one of the South's "peculiar institutions."

In contrast, the North has been declared "born free." Farmers, we like to believe, owned title to their land, and the yeoman farmer was the dominant figure on the rural landscape. From Crèvecoeur to Jefferson to William Jennings Bryan, writers reinforced this image of our heritage.[7]

In this instance, however, myth does not square with historical fact. Indeed, from their earliest settlement, agricultural land in important sections of the United States—including Western New York—were worked by men and women who had no title to the land and who passed on a significant share of its product to absentee landlords.[8]

From the beginning of settlement in New York, large land companies, like the Holland Land Company, held title to the land, in many cases sparking resentment from disgruntled settlers. In November 1819, for example, at a meeting in Genesee County "the extravagant prices demanded by the Holland Land Company were condemned, the amount of money being drained from the county by the payment of the principal and interest was deplored, and the participants recommended that steps be taken to require foreign owners to provide their fair share of taxes for roads and schools."[9]

According to Gates, "permanent landlordism flourished" in western New York. "Here men of capital determined to erect for themselves and their families estates to be held in perpetuity. Land was sold only to raise essential capital for further improvements on other land or because it was undesirable to hold certain remote or separate tracts. . . . Landlords had no difficulty in securing tenants or in making agreements with squatters already on their land."[10]

The difference between owners and tenants was not trivial. Rent was a considerable cost; its payment prevented tenants from accumulating the capital needed to buy their own farm. According to U. P. Hendrick, in New York as in the South, sharecropping, not money rent, was common. The share due the landowner, if he supplied animals, tools, and seeds, often went as high as two-thirds of the year's harvest. If supplies were not included, the share was still one-half.[11]

Tenancy was an important feature of the social structure of Erie County. According to the 1855 state census, one in five rural household heads in the county was a tenant. Nor were tenants simply young men waiting to gather sufficient equity to buy a farm; they were distributed across the age structure. From its earliest settlement, Erie County had a permanent tenant population.

Was the division between owner and tenant important? The relationship between consciousness and objective economic divisions, of course, is neither constant nor predictable. Echoing the debate over Populism, historians do not know if America's farmers were mobility-conscious entrepreneurs, rebellious peasants, or democratically motivated yeoman.[12]

One measure of the impact of social structure on consciousness, however, is differences in family strategy. If tenant farmers made the same decisions concerning the timing and structure of their families as owners, then the case of a distinct class division is diminished. If, on the other hand, clear divisions existed between the family processes of the two groups, the case for the importance of class distinctions is strengthened. The fertility of Erie County farmers, then, provides a test for the convergence of consciousness and objective conditions in rural America.

Differential Fertility in Rural Erie County

The data on Erie County farmers in 1855 is particularly rich. In addition to the population census we have used in earlier chapters, farm families were linked to the agricultural census, which provides an immense amount of information on the rural farm economy. For our investigation, a number of variables are particularly important: acres improved and unimproved, farm value, and the value of stock, tools, and implements, and total farm capital.

Given its history, tenancy had a significance in rural Erie County that it did not have in Buffalo. In the city, property ownership was primarily an object of consumption. As Katz, Doucet, and Stern discovered, most urban families were interested in property for its "use-value," the shelter and security it provided. While property was important to the family economy, it was not capital, a means of generating wealth.[13]

This was not the case in the countryside. There, land was unambiguously a capital investment. Owners could carry out their vocation and keep the returns on their investment, while tenants were forced to surrender a substantial proportion of their crop either as a share or cash rent.

In short, rural Erie County had a two-class social structure. But unlike the city, where class was defined by the contrast between businessmen's and workers' jobs, in the countryside social class was defined along property lines.

Of course, class is not simply a property relationship. It represents the process through which economic differences are translated into differences in social life, including life chances, authority relationships, and patterns of consumption and distribution. If the class "structuration" of Erie County were weak, the formal distinction between owner and renter would not create differences in these other aspects of life, including fertility. Conversely, if social class differences in fertility were great, it suggests that the "class principle" was strong.[14]

Among Erie County's native-born farmers, class differences in fertility were strong and important. Yet among the other major ethnic group, the Germans, no similar differentials can be identified. To understand this, we must delve into the German farmers' life experience and the sense they made of it.

The fertility of Erie County farm wives in 1855 was ten percent higher than that of Buffalo. Much of the difference was among women over the age of 30. Thus, family limitation was less common in the countryside than in the city.

Birthplace was an important determinant of fertility in the countryside in 1855 (Table 5.1). While the Irish and Canadians were important parts of the social structure of Buffalo, only the Germans were common in rural Erie County. Their fertility was almost always higher than that of native-born farm wives. At the same time, German farm fertility was greater than that of urban Germans. In every age cohort, the German farmers had higher fertility, for some as much as eighty percent.

The age-specific fertility patterns of native-born and German farmers were distinct as well. Starting with a ratio of 1,261 per thousand for German-born women aged 20–24, their fertility ratio climbed to 1,635

Table 5.1. Standardized Fertility Ratio, by Birthplace and Age, Erie County Farmers, 1855

Birthplace	20–49	20–24	25–29	30–34	35–39	40–44	45–49	N
			Women's Age					
New England	940	1,242	845	1,226	1,464	430	149	(98)
New York State	920	1,051	973	989	1,119	918	308	(378)
Other United States	667	1,000	1,000	1,200	333	59	476	(36)
Ireland	926	1,500	1,478	250	1,375	1,000	0	(15)
Other United Kingdom	692	500	1,214	182	1,750	71	0	(24)
Germany	1,434	1,261	1,635	2,207	1,215	1,234	687	(284)
Other	660	950	95	1,000	250	1,000	455	(16)

SOURCE: Calculated from New York State Census manuscripts 1855.

and then 2,207 per thousand among women between the ages of 25 and 34. Even among German-born women in their late thirties and early forties, the fertility ratio remained above 1,200 per thousand.

The fertility ratio of native-born women was lower across the life cycle, but it did not vary as much with age. While it never rose as high as the German ratio, it remained near 1,000 per thousand until the 45–49 years age-cohort.

In Europe and Colonial America, fertility had been regulated by restrictions on marriage. As J. Hajnal noted, it was the late marriage age and high celibacy rate of European peasants that led to their low overall fertility, not low marital fertility. When the marital fertility decline did come to Europe, it was associated with the "family limitation" pattern— high early peak and concave decline—identified by van de Walle and Knodel.[15]

This was not the case among American farmers. By 1855, native farmers had achieved relatively low marital fertility without family limitation. They were not attempting to limit their family to a specific size, but they were apparently lengthening the interval between births as a means of reducing their completed fertility.

The fertility experience of native-born farm families in Erie County fits the "land-availability" model. As the second generation of settlers in the county, they were the first families to face a depleted land market. With little new unimproved land at their disposal, native farmers faced declining expectations. Unless they were willing to relocate to the new frontier beyond the Mississippi, they had few opportunities to expand their holdings or those of their children. The declining availability of land may have led to fertility restriction.

If this theory were correct, why did the German farmers not restrict their fertility? Here again, the objective economic situation must be evaluated in terms of historical experience.

The Germans who migrated to America during the nineteenth century were, for the most part, refugees from the crumbling peasant economy of central Europe. A combination of demographic and economic jolts swept the region, bringing with them an explosion in rural proletarianization and the wholesale eviction of peasants from their holdings. "The number of these smallholders, and of entirely landless peasants," according to Jerome Blum, "grew prodigiously in the great demographic upsurge that began in the eighteenth century."[16] Those farmers who remained saw their holdings shrink. For example, in the Hochberg region of Baden, according to Blum, 45 percent of the population held less than 1.8 acres and another 39 percent held between 1.8 and 7.2 acres. Only five percent held more than 14.4 acres.

Compared to these holdings, the German farmers of Erie County were flush. While 26 percent of the German-born population reported no land holdings, 44 percent of the Germans worked over twenty acres. The Germans—on average poorer than native-born farmers—were rich by European standards.

Economic conditions were not simple facts that had a direct impact on fertility. They were mediated by the cultural meaning that social groups attributed to them. Poverty or land scarcity were not easily measured quantities, but filtered through individuals' life experience. In a social context in which that experience was so varied, interpretations and behaviors too were distinctively different.

Fertility was negatively correlated with economic standing among Erie County farmers (Table 5.2). Using farm value, those farmers who were in the bottom sixty percent of the population had average fertility ratios between 1,148 and 1,221 per thousand, while the ratio for the top forty percent was around 900 per thousand. The relationship of value of stock, tools, and instruments, and total capital to fertility was similar. The number of acres was less correlated with fertility, probably because of variation in land quality.

As we have suggested, social class in Erie County was defined by land tenure. Tenants had a fertility ratio twelve percent above that of

Table 5.2. Standardized Fertility Ratio, by Percentile Distribution Value of Farm, Stock, Tools and Implements, and Total Capital, Erie County, 1855

Economic	Percentile					
Measure	0–19%	20–39%	40–59%	60–79%	80–89%	90–99%
Farm value	1,143	1,192	1,221	909	892	876
Stock value	1,133	1,178	1,127	1,013	873	1,048
Tools and implements value	1,072	1,188	1,326	974	1,055	979
Total capital	1,147	1,223	1,247	907	870	944

Total N = 867

SOURCE: Calculated from New York Census manuscript.

Table 5.3. Standardized Fertility Ratio, by Length of Residence, Property Ownership, Improved and Unimproved Acres, Erie County Farmers, 1855

Variable	N	Fertility Ratio
Length of Residence		
Less than 1 year	40	908
1–4 years	199	1,138
5–9 years	163	1,283
10–14 years	63	1,385
15–19 years	82	859
20 years and over	318	999
Property Ownership		
Tenants	156	1,226
Owners	711	1,081
Improved Acres		
None	169	1,174
1–19	156	1,116
20–39	189	1,097
40–69	174	1,066
70–89	91	775
90 and over	88	1,034
Unimproved Acres		
None	222	1,152
1–9	109	1,274
10–24	179	1,109
25–39	144	852
40–59	108	1,165
60 and over	105	870

SOURCE: Calculated from New York State Census manuscripts.

owners (Table 5.3). Thus, at the very least, the two groups had distinct fertility strategies.

Yet these data mask the complex interaction of fertility and social class with migration and economic standing. Among the tenants, for example, length of residence and fertility were negatively related—long-term tenants had fewer children (Table 5.4). The fertility ratio of those tenants who had lived in the county for less than five years was more than twice that of those who had lived there for fifteen years or longer. Among owners, however, there was no clear relationship. With the exception of the low fertility of the newest owners, the migration cohorts had similar fertility ratios.

The data suggest that tenants' fertility was more influenced by economic conditions than was owners'. For example, if we control for land tenure, fertility is generally unrelated to dwelling value or total farm capital for owners, but strongly related for tenants. The mildly negative

Table 5.4. Standardized Fertility Ratio, by Percentile Distribution of Property Ownership, Dwelling Value, and Total Capital, and by Length of Residence, Erie County Farmers, 1855.

Variable	N	Tenants	N	Owners
Dwelling Value				
0–19%	34	1,238	123	1,076
20–39%	43	1,658	124	1,095
40–59%	18	979	105	1,157
60–79%	30	1,422	173	1,147
80–89%	16	827	91	981
90–99%	14	88	96	901
Total Capital				
0–19%	82	1,416	86	903
20–39%	16	1,203	159	1,062
40–59%	17	1,195	155	1,264
60–79%	22	842	153	898
80–89%	8	162	79	1,028
90–99%	12	629	79	1,004
Length of Residence				
Less than 1 year	17	1,310	23	637
1–4 years	56	1,361	143	1,061
5–9 years	30	1,124	133	1,321
10–14 years	10	1,207	53	1,377
15–19 years	4	567	78	865
20 years and over	38	647	281	1,034

SOURCE: Calculated from New York State Census manuscripts.

relationship between these variables for the entire population, then, was a product of their strong correlation for tenants diluted by the weak relationship among owners. Among owners, some fertility restriction was common regardless of economic standing, but among renters it was related to the specific economic situation of the family.

The class differentials in fertility did not cross ethnic lines. German tenants and German owners had similar fertility ratios. Among natives, however, the gap was large. Owners' fertility was fourteen percent less than that of tenants (Table 5.5).

Germans and natives also reacted to length of residence differently.

Table 5.5. Standardized Fertility Ratio, by Birthplace and Length of Residence, Dwelling Value, Property Ownership, and Total Capital, Erie County Farmers, 1855

	Birthplace	
Variable	United States	Germany
(N)	(512)	(284)
Length of Residence		
Less than 1 year	987	675
1–4 years	1,032	1,251
5–9 years	748	1,388
10–14 years	1,257	1,519
15–19 years	633	1,933
20 years and over	880	1,464
Dwelling Value		
0–19% percentile	1,121	1,412
20–39% percentile	976	1,414
40–59% percentile	1,096	1,339
60–79% percentile	759	1,978
80–89% percentile	821	1,077
90–99% percentile	754	1,365
Property Ownership		
Tenants	998	1,477
Owners	876	1,450
Total Capital		
0–19% percentile	943	1,181
20–39% percentile	1,058	1,527
40–59% percentile	990	1,653
60–79% percentile	686	1,448
80–89% percentile	723	867
90–99% percentile	893	547

SOURCE: Calculated from New York State Census manuscripts.

Among newcomers, German fertility was actually lower than that of native-born farm families, while among long-time residents, the German ratio outstripped the native by as much as fifty percent. If Germans were "acculturating," it did not affect their fertility. The longer farmers had been in Erie County, the less likely they were to conform to U.S. natives' fertility patterns.

Because of the complexity of these relationships, we have used a multivariate statistical technique, multiple classification analysis, to sort out the independent influence of each of these factors. Age at marriage, property ownership, birthplace, dwelling value, and total farm capital all had statistically significant influences on fertility; length of residence, when controlled for other factors, did not.[17]

As in Buffalo, ethnicity and social class remained the major social determinants of fertility. In the county, however, these influences were more contingent. Land tenure influenced fertility only among native farm families; among Germans it was not important. At the same time, economic standing interacted with land tenure and ethnicity. Owners were not influenced by economic standing, while tenants were.

Conclusion

Much of the research on fertility in rural America has been concerned with regional differentials in fertility and their relationship to land availability. While Yasuba's thesis remains controversial, neither its advocates nor critics have been able to develop a plausible historical explanation linking the two factors.

Given this impasse, the examination of intraregional fertility differentials is in order. The European and American literature agrees that social structure and culture each had a powerful impact on urban fertility. Why shouldn't these same factors affect farm fertility?

In Erie County, these forces were indeed important. Owners had lower fertility than tenants. Immigrants had higher fertility than natives. Most intriguing, economic standing influenced fertility among tenants, but had relatively little influence among owners.

Among Europeans, rural proletarianization was a significant determinant of fertility change. The proletarianizing of the rural work force there during the eighteenth and nineteenth centuries weakened collective controls on marriage and caused a fertility explosion.[18]

Proletarianization obviously was not an important determinant of fertility in America, where the rural landless were a relatively small proportion of the population. The split between owners and tenants, however, was a crucial influence on individuals' life chances and family strategies.

Land owners reaped the full reward of their labor, but had to worry about the disposal of their land and its division among their children. Tenants had to pass a significant share of their product to their landlords. At the same time, with nothing to pass on to their children, they may have been less concerned with the impact of family size on inheritance. At least among the native-born, owners restricted fertility more than tenants.

While their overall fertility was low, native-born landholders did not practice family limitation. Rather, they reduced fertility across the woman's life cycle through birth spacing. As with some populations in the city of Buffalo, birth spacing served as a transitional strategy between unrestricted fertility and the family limitation of the future.

Yet the economic imperative to limit fertility was imbedded in particular cultural outlooks. German farmers, while not as well off as the natives, showed no compunction to limit fertility. Not only was their fertility higher, but the longer they had lived in Erie County, the higher it was.

Fleeing the agricultural revolution sweeping central Europe, the Germans seemed to find their holdings in Erie County of sufficient size to support a large family. Even the tenant–owner split, so important among natives, made little difference for the Germans.

Erie County's fertility patterns give limited support to the land-availability thesis. While it is plausible that landholders were limiting their fertility to mitigate the problems of inheritance and partibility, we might expect that the less-well-off farmers would be most likely to limit their fertility. The fact that the richest families had the lowest fertility suggests that other factors may have been equally important.

Yet, at the same time that these data give some support to Yasuba's thesis, they demonstrate its methodological and conceptual limits. By stressing interregional differences, the participants in the land-availability debate have ignored the impact of social structure on fertility, particularly the role of land tenure.

From its earliest settlement, the social structure of rural America, including western New York, was marked by sharp differences between owners and tenants. These divisions, reinforced by variations in wealth, capital, and size of holding, significantly affected the life chances of farm families and the fertility strategies they formulated.

Ultimately, the family strategy of most rural Americans did not work. Depopulation and the farmers' revolt of the late nineteenth century were the demographic and political legacy of that failure. Perhaps if we pay more attention to the attempts of families to cope with the economic currents of the mid-nineteenth century, we will better understand their failure and its wider implications for American history.[19]

We can also gain perspective on urban fertility patterns from an examination of the rural data. As in the city, shifts in the opportunity structure and cultural patterns made up the force field in which fertility strategies took shape. The class differences between tenants and owners interacted with the historical experience of the county's ethnic groups to define clear fertility differentials. This combination of objective conditions and cultural interpretation structured the social definition of fertility.

6

Conclusion: Fertility and Social History

THE small family pattern swept through Erie County and the nation between 1855 and 1915. Fertility rates fell for virtually every group in the population: businessmen and workers, natives and immigrants, schooled and unschooled.

Yet in the midst of this general decline, persistent patterns remained. The same occupational differentials visible in 1855 were still present in 1915, while the relationship of fertility to foreign birth and length of residence remained. High-school attendance was related to fertility both at the group and individual level. Finally, the same factors that influenced urban fertility were important among rural populations.

I have argued that the decline of fertility can be understood as a complex outcome of the interaction of social structure and culture. The primary change in the social structure was the nationalization of the U.S. economy under the auspices of private corporations. This restructuring of the economy altered the opportunity structure and family economy.

The rise of the corporation had two impacts on opportunity. First, the managerial revolution created a new stratum of white-collar workers. The specialized professionals and business employees became the growth sector of the business class, attracting the sons (and later the daughters) of the old business and working classes.

Second, the new corporations' strategies of control dictated a split labor market. A primary stratum of well-off skilled workers had better wages, more security, and a safer work place, while the secondary working-class stratum still labored under the terrible conditions of the past.

The opportunity structure altered the contours of family strategy. For the business class, the decline of entrepreneurial employment encouraged, first, the new business stratum and, then, the old business stratum to direct their children to the professions and business employment.

Among workers, these imperatives were reinforced by the decline in poverty among the upper-tier worker families. The decline of structural poverty, on the one hand, provided the material resources to prolong children's time in school and, on the other hand, added a predictability to the family life cycle. Taken together, the better-off workers of the early twentieth century were confronted with a new set of social conditions that encouraged them to change their family life: to consume more, keep their children in school, and limit their fertility.

The social structural determinants of fertility were mediated by cultural influences. Sharp ethnic fertility differentials were their most conspicuous expression, but more subtle pressures were also visible. Within ethnic groups, there was great diversity in fertility levels, tied to such factors as intermarriage, generational differences, and the timing of migration. Culture channeled and controlled the impact of social structure.

In most respects, the fertility transition in Erie County conforms to the portrait of the new demographic theorists. With Caldwell, I have stressed the impact of family strategy and the subtle interaction of family economy and ideology. I have also endorsed Lestaeghe's insistence on the importance of social control. Finally, with Knodel and van de Walle, I have found that fertility decline was "innovative" behavior, linked to the distinctive patterns of family limitation.

At the same time, there are some weaknesses in these earlier formulations. While innovation was the dominant pattern in fertility decline, our data challenge the neat division between family limitation and traditional methods of fertility restriction. While some groups seem to have moved directly from high, unrestricted to low, restricted fertility, others may have used traditional fertility restriction—especially birth spacing—as a half-way house on the way to family limitation.

The fertility decline in Erie County also qualifies Caldwell's interpretation of the impact of education on fertility. While Caldwell concedes that education had a direct economic impact on fertility, for him its primary importance was in breaking the legitimacy of the traditional family ideology. Education, for Caldwell, liberated working-class youths from the selfish demands of their parents.

In Erie County, parental resistence to education did not seem to be motivated simply by self-interest. While those families in poverty may have sacrificed their children's ultimate success for short-term family survival, when these economic constraints were relaxed they quickly embraced prolonged education and lower fertility. The changing opportunity structure and family economy were more important to the education revolution than was the breakdown of family ideology.

Finally, this study underlines the wisdom of investigating the middle range of social institutions. The dualism of the "individual" and "society" cannot capture the dynamism of social action. Examining the theory of the demographic transition, one is tempted to insist that families, not "societies," limit their fertility. If we turn to the economic theory of fertility, however, we want to shout that world view and social values are more than merely individual "tastes" and "preferences."

Social class and ethnicity provide the link between these concepts. In an environment of shared material circumstances, life experiences, and beliefs, the members of these groups forged distinctive patterns of understanding and behavior. The fertility decline is part of the "structuration" of advanced societies.[1]

While the causes of the fertility decline are important, we must guard against becoming obsessed with them. It is wrong to separate the fertility decline from the more general course of American social history during the late nineteenth and early twentieth centuries. Therefore, in this conclusion, I want to turn the arrows in the model around, to examine how the study of fertility illuminates some of the broader issues in the history of American society.

In *The Social Organization of Early Industrial Capitalism*, Michael Katz, Michael Doucet, and I asserted baldly that a "two-class model describes not only the objective relations of early industrial cities but the perception of their principal interpreters as well." As we hoped, this attempt to rise above the sheer bulk of quantitative analysis and draw some conclusions about the nature of American society has drawn fire from across the ideological spectrum.[2]

Yet, the smoke we have generated has often obscured the historical point we were making. An older generation of Marxists wanted to demonstrate that the United States, because it is a capitalist society, was, is, and always will be a two-class society. Nothing could be farther from our intention.

The two-class structure of mid-nineteenth-century American cities represented simply a given moment in our history. Earlier, the "stratification from below" of artisans had preserved a middle class of skilled workers and small proprietors. Later, the "stratification from above" divided the working class between primary and secondary strata. As we noted in the conclusion, "at the start of the twentieth century . . . class structure had grown more complex."[3]

Anthony Giddens, who was a major source for our ideas about social class, has noted that "a threefold class structure is generic to capitalist society." Yet, he goes on to note, "the mode in which these elements are merged to form *a specific class system*, in any given society, differs significantly according to variations in economic and political development."[4]

The two-class structure of the mid-nineteenth-century city was volatile. It was prone to crisis and social schism. Indeed, the "search for order" of the late nineteenth-century was, in part, an effort to reduce the tensions inherent in this social formation.[5]

The new family strategies embraced by most members of the society were an important part of the "remaking" of class relations. Among business-class families, the small family became, along with new standards of consumption and culture, a means of binding together the disparate parts of the class. While the structural realities of the new and old business classes diverged, these commonalities in the world of consumption kept them together socially.

Among workers, the impact of the new family strategy was more ambiguous. On the one hand, the declining poverty, improved opportunities, and new family strategy of the upper tier of the working class made the lives of its members more comfortable and increased their acceptance of the existing social order. On the other hand, they did not become "middle class." In Stedman Jones's phrase, the working class was not abolished, but "remade."[6]

The new family strategy did much to undercut the collective reality of the working class in space and time. A new level of consumption pulled workers and their families away from the collective elements of culture— the tavern, the fraternal organization, and the street—and deposited them in the family home. From Bethnal Green to Boston's West End, improved material circumstances threatened street–corner society.[7]

At the same time, the new calculations of working class life—schooling for the kids, consumer goods for mom, a vacation from work for dad— worked against the assumption of responsibility for wider kin networks.

The use of kinship for trading, gift giving, and borrowing was an essential strategy for "risk sharing" in the uncertain life of poverty. As families began to see a way to get out of deprivation, they were less likely to let wider responsibilities pull them back.[8]

Yet simple models of embourgeoisement do not work. While a major cultural frontier was crossed by many families, they did so in a social structure still dominated by the business class, one in which anti-union laws, repression, and coercion were still facts of working-class life.

To capture the complexity of class relations in the early twentieth century, we must move beyond the models of open conflict or consensual acceptance that have dominated American history. Rather, as T. J. Jackson Lear suggests, Antonio Gramsci's concept of cultural hegemony is useful for capturing the dynamics of accommodation and resistance.

While workers continued to be subordinate to businessmen in the work place, in their everyday life they gave "spontaneous consent . . . to the general direction imposed on social life by the dominant fundamental group." Yet this acceptance had its limits. At the same time that they accepted "middle-class" standards of consumption and family life, workers could openly confront the business class in politics and the work place. The "line between dominant and subordinate cultures is a permeable membrane, not an impenetrable barrier."[9]

The decline of fertility and the remaking of the working-class family, then, added a new dimension of complexity to class relations in early-twentieth-century America. It subverted the collective institutions that were at the center of nineteenth century working-class life, but at the same time, it created a new set of expectations on the part of working-class families, expectations of improved chances for social mobility and higher standards of living.

The history of fertility decline in Erie County sheds light also on the process of social and cultural change. "Modernization" theory—of which the theory of the demographic transition is a part—has stressed the gradual, evolutionary nature of family change. The family, according to Ernest Burgess, Harvey Locke, and Mary Thomes, "has been in transition from a traditional family system, based on family members playing traditional roles, to a companionship family system, based on mutual affection, intimate communication, and mutual acceptance of the division of labor and procedures of decision-making."[10]

The evolutionary models of social change can be attacked on purely conceptual grounds. Whether functionalist or not, the use of organic metaphors does not capture the subtle interplay between subjectivity and objective social conditions. As Giddens has noted: "Human history does not have an evolutionary 'shape,' and positive harm can be done by attempting to compress it into one."[11]

The case of Erie County challenges the evolutionary model of family change. While the fertility rate in Erie County and the nation may have slowly edged down, if we examine the experience of different groups, we find sharp discontinuities in the county's fertility experience. Groups resisted the decline in fertility and prolonged school attendance for a long time, indeed. Then, in a few years, behavior suddenly changed.

The inadequacy of the evolutionary model recommends a concept of social change that emphasizes discontinuities. Here, Thomas Kuhn's well-known model of scientific revolutions is suggestive. Rather than being an evolutionary process, for Kuhn scientific history is marked by sharp breaks during which one paradigm is replaced by another.[12]

Kuhn's model, which has been one of the hottest intellectual properties of the past decade, posits a cycle of cultural change. A crisis develops as the existing paradigm encounters nagging problems and inconsistencies. During the crisis a number of paradigms compete for hegemony. Then after a dominant paradigm emerges, a period of rationalization ("normal science") completes the revolution.

Anthony Wallace has already proposed a similar "paradigmatic" approach to cultural change, although he has stayed close to Kuhn in focusing on technological innovation. Glen Elder, following W. I. Thomas, has used a model of social change and the family which is very similar to Kuhn's.[13]

The process of family change is quite similar to that of scientific revolution. "Habitual patterns of behavior are maintained," writes Elder, "by situations in which the group or individual is able to produce outcomes that are in line with expectations or claims." Yet, in a crisis, this system fails to work: "a sharp disparity between claims and control, between cultural patterns and resulting situational definitions, and the resources to achieve desired benefits" develops. New patterns emerge in an effort "to restore control over one's life or destiny, but under terms of the new situation."[14]

The process of family change must then be approached in its totality. Not only do specific "variables" change, but their configuration and meaning are also altered in the cycle of crisis, innovation, and routinization. Any individual factor must be viewed in relationship to the entire ensemble of behaviors. Rather than being predictive, "this model of inquiry centers on the historical events or change and examines the process through which it finds expression in family patterns, life experience, and social character."[15]

At midcentury, the working-class family of Erie County had an identifiable strategy that utilized high fertility, child labor, and boarding as a means of assuring the family's survival in a context of uncertainty and deprivation. That context, however, did not remain stable. The declining market for unskilled youth labor, the expansion of relevant educational opportunities, the improved economic situation of the family, and the crusades of middle-class "child savers" threw the old system into crisis.

In the years before the First World War, working-class families experimented with new family processes. But if a new family strategy were to be adopted, a number of its elements would have to be restructured. If families were to prolong the education of their children and improve their own material standards, fertility would need to be reduced. Despite the profound character of these changes, a large proportion of Erie County families carried them out in just a few years.

The linchpin to the new family strategy was the decline of predictable life-cycle poverty, a change which opened up a set of choices that had previously been closed. Earlier, the lack of resources made it "irrational" to devote much time to long-range planning. With so few resources and little control, such an effort would have been little more than daydreaming.

The improved material situation of the working-class family changed its "horizon of planning." Through most of the nineteenth century, economic constraints severely limited this horizon. "Under the compelling requirements of economic survival," Elder notes, "rationales for adaptation are apt to be highly restricted in scope and time perspective. . . . An emergency situation implies that short-run considerations outweigh the potential consequences of action for the future welfare of the family or individuals."[16]

Thus, the increase in the working-class standard of living had two impacts on its families' strategies. First, the family's material constraints were reduced. Children no longer had to be pulled from school. Boarders no longer had to be crammed into spare corners of the family's dwelling. Second, psychologically the improved economic situation of the family made long-range planning possible. With an enhanced perception of control, working-class parents could think about the future in a way that would have been foolish earlier.

Elder's study of the Great Depression also raises the issue of the psychological impact of social change. Giddens argues, consistent with Elder, that social change initiates a process of denial, regression, adjustment, and routinization on the part of the individual. But Giddens's examples come from situations of decremental change—Le Bon's analysis of the crowd, Bettelheim's of concentration camp victims. We might ask if the same process affects situations in which material conditions improve?[17]

A complex understanding of the nature of social change has implications, as well, for the history of immigration in America. Oscar Handlin's story of immigrant adjustment fits very well with Giddens's analysis. For Handlin, the combined impact of the passage from Europe and conditions in the New World stripped the immigrants of their old culture. A period of disorientation marked by crime, psychological breakdown, and amorality was followed by the emergence of a new "American" culture.[18]

Herbert Gutman and Virginia Yans-McLaughlin, among others, have attacked this model, focusing instead on the ability of immigrant groups to retain their cultural preferences in the face of capitalist imperatives. Yet, as we saw in Chapter Four, Yans-McLaughlin has been taken to task—in my view justly—for minimizing the structural impacts on immigrant work patterns. Gabriel Kolko, meanwhile, has moved beyond Handlin, claiming that the children of the immigrants found themselves *without* a culture, caught between a thin, peasant culture they never really knew and a mainline American culture that was not open to them.[19]

The evidence from Erie County does not provide any final answers to these issues. New patterns emerged as older ones broke down. We cannot go along with Yans-McLaughlin's notion of a pristine immigrant culture warding off American standards, yet the evidence of ethnic diversity cannot be ignored. Rather than posing it as a "did they or didn't they" question, it is wiser to focus on the process of change and ask *when* they did and *when* they didn't.

The family history of Erie County between 1855 and 1920, finally, provides perspective on the American family's experience during this century. As we have seen, some of the major aspects of family life fell into place during this period—low fertility, prolonged school attendance, the emergence of the male as the primary "breadwinner." Yet, while these elements of the "modern" American family became common during the 1910s, the Great Depression and its severe impact on family life interrupted their development.

The family life of deprived families during the Depression, as described by Elder, was similar to that of families before the fertility transition. The wages of the male household head were no longer sufficient. Children were pulled from school and sent to work. Women sought to take in boarders.

The response of families to the Great Depression, then, was not at all new. The family strategy of deprived families was the reactivation of a strategy that had well served working-class families less than a half-century earlier. Indeed, the severity of the psychological trauma for middle-class families noted by Elder may have been a result of their lack of this resource. While the working class still had a set of patterns in mind for economic crisis, the middle class was wholly unprepared for it.[20]

A century-long view also provides an ironic perspective on the post-Second World War generation. According to Elder, the signs of family change "among the offspring of deprived families are consistently in a conservative direction, toward traditional values and relationships. Traditional family preferences among women are related to childhood experiences in economically deprived households."[21]

Note that in this passage Elder equates "traditional" and "conservative." Although such an equation makes sense in modernization theory—for which the direction and meaning of change are fixed—it makes little sense in a "crisis and innovation" framework. If any family form was "traditional" in 1940 it was the nineteenth-century (and Depression) pattern with its emphasis on the productive role of women and children.

The family strategy premised on the husband as provider and wife and children as consumers—what Barbara Ehrenreich calls the "family wage-system"—was a relatively new innovation, one that emerged in the working class only around the turn of the century. The family strategy that the children of the Great Depression adopted was not "traditional" in a temporal sense. Rather, the "family-centered" pattern of the 1950s was the first extended use of a strategy which had only been tested briefly during the first several decades of the twentieth century.[22]

This strategy was conservative, however, and here lies a problem that continues to bother students of the family. Whether in poverty or affluence, from the mid-nineteenth century until today, American families have demonstrated a clear conservatism. Not conservatism in a narrow political sense or in hostility to change. Rather, families have been conservative in their attempt to maintain the integrity of family values in the face of "outside" demands. Much of the resistance to campaigns for moral reform—from the attack on lodgers in the early twentieth century through the "family protection" movement of the 1980s—has been based on a belief that they would restrict the autonomy and self-determination of the family. The death of the "haven in a heartless world" may have been exaggerated.[23]

The history of family limitation remains the story of individual families making sense of the crises of everyday life. Conservatives who wish to see it as the subversion of the "traditional" family, and feminists who want to believe it represents a politicizing of everyday life, are both likely to misread its motivation and its outcome.

This study concludes, then, with a contradiction. From the perspective of society, the decline of fertility was a means through which the family accommodated itself to the existing social order. If we view it from the standpoint of the family, however, fertility limitation was one of the ways that the family attempted to protect itself from the intrusion of the larger society.

The dualism between the macro- and micro-social may be better expressed as a duality. The "society" from which families attempted to insulate themselves was reproduced through their actions. At the same time, the "family values" they wished to protect were not some age-old belief but the product of relatively recent attempts to cope with social change.

The "meaning" of the decline in fertility does not afford us any simple conclusions about the American family—past, present, or future. The comforting images of increased autonomy, more rationality, and more concern for individuals are balanced by those of a family turned into the agent of the powers-that-be, devoid of autonomy, and producing individuals without conscience or respect.

We may share Richard Hofstadter's sympathies for those who want "to believe that somewhere in the American past there was a golden age whose life was far better than our own," or others' wish to project such a world into the future. Yet the lessons of the past and the prospects of the future do not afford us that luxury.

Notes

Introduction

1. Quoted in Richard Easterlin, "The Economics and Sociology of Fertility: A Synthesis," in Charles Tilly, *Historical Studies in Changing Fertility* (Princeton, N.J., 1978), pp. 57–134.
2. Anthony F. C. Wallace, *Rockdale: The Growth of an American Village in the Early Industrial Revolution* (New York, 1978), pp. 477–486.
3. Michael B. Katz, *The People of Hamilton, Canada West, Class and Family in a Mid-Nineteenth Century City* (Cambridge, Mass., 1975) p. ix.

1 Explaining the Decline in Fertility

1. Quoted in Lee Rainwater, *And the Poor Get Children: Sex, Contraception, and Family Planning in the Working Class* (Chicago, 1960), p. 19.
2. R. B. Tabbarah, "Toward a Theory of Demographic Development," *Economic Development and Social Change* 19 (1971), pp. 257–277; Easterlin, "The Economics and Sociology of Fertility."
3. J. Hajnal, "The European Marriage Pattern in Perspective," in David V. Glass and D. E. C Eversley, eds., *Population in History: Essays in Historical Demography* (London, 1965), pp. 101–146.
4. Gerard Bouchard, *Le village immobile: Sennely-en-Sologne au XVIIIe siecle* (Paris, 1972). Cited in Edward Shorter, *The Making of the Modern Family* (London, 1976), p. 26.
5. Phillip Greven, *Four Generations: Population, Land, and Family in Colonial Andover, Massachusetts* (Ithaca, N.Y., 1970), p. 105. At the beginning of the eighteenth century, the ratio of marriages to births was 1:7.6 in Andover.

6. Jacques Henripin, *Trends and Factors of Fertility in Canada* (Ottawa, 1972), pp. 9–10.

7. W. H. Grabrill, C. V. Kiser, and P. K. Whelpton, *The Fertility of American Women* (New York, 1958).

8. Ansley J. Coale and Marvin Zelnick, *New Estimates of Fertility and Population in the United States* (Princeton, N.J., 1963).

9. Coale and Zelnick, pp. 34–35.

10. P. K. Whelpton, "Industrial Development and Population Growth," *Social Forces* 6 (March and June 1928).

11. Yasukichi Yasuba, *Birth Rates of the White Population in the United States, 1800–1860* (Baltimore, 1962).

12. Wendell Bash, "Changing Birth Rates in Developing America: New York State, 1840–1875," *The Milbank Memorial Fund Quarterly* 41 (1963), pp. 161–182; D. R. Leet, "Human Fertility and Agricultural Opportunities in Ohio Counties: From Frontier to Maturity, 1810–1860," in D. C. Klingaman and R. K. Velder, eds., *Essays in Nineteenth Century Economic History: The Old Northwest* (Athens, Ohio, 1975); John Modell, "Family and Fertility on the Indiana Frontier, 1820," *American Quarterly* 23 (1971), pp. 615–634; Colin Forster and G. S. L. Tucker, *Economic Opportunity and White Fertility Ratios* (New Haven, Conn., 1972).

13. Richard Easterlin, George Alter, and Gretchen A. Condran, "Farm Families in Old and New Areas: The Northern States in 1860," in Tamara K. Hareven and Maris A. Vinovskis, eds., *Family and Population in Nineteenth-Century America* (Princeton, N.J., 1978), pp. 22–85.

14. Richard A. Easterlin, "Factors in the Decline of Farm Family Fertility in the United States: Some Preliminary Research Results," *Journal of American History* 63 (1976), pp. 600–614. Easterlin, Alter, and Condran define settlement by the number of ever-improved acres per township improved by 1860. Their analysis does not have to contend with the problems of multicolinearity between urbanization and high population density that troubled earlier researchers who used aggregate level data.

15. Greven, *Four Generations*.

16. Maris A. Vinovskis, "Socio-economic Determinants of Interstate Fertility Differentials in the United States in 1850 and 1860," *Journal of Interdisciplinary History* 6 (1976), pp. 375–396, and "A Multivariate Regression Analysis of Fertility Differentials among Massachusetts Townships and Regions in 1860," in Tilly, ed., *Historical Studies of Changing Fertility*, pp. 225–256.

17. Maris A. Vinovskis, *Fertility in Massachusetts from the Revolution to the Civil War* (New York, 1981), p. 150.

18. Tamara K. Hareven and Maris A. Vinovskis, "Marital Fertility, Ethnicity, and Occupation in Urban Families: An Analysis of South Boston and the South End in 1880," *Journal of Social History* 8 (1975), pp. 69–93; and "Patterns of Childbearing in Late-Nineteenth Century America: The Determinants of Marital Fertility in Five Massachusetts Towns in 1880," in their *Family and Population*, pp. 85–125.

19. Hareven and Vinovskis, "Patterns of Childbearing," pp. 124–125.

20. See Michael B. Katz, *The People of Hamilton*, pp. 139–140, on occupational classification in the 19th century. Another problem which we shall discuss below is the inference of longitudinal trends from cross-sectional data. In Hamilton, Ontario, between 1851 and 1871, occupational fertility changed from a pattern in which the business class had the higher fertility to one in which the working class did. Captured at one point in time, this pattern appeared to demonstrate that occupation was not a "determinant" of fertility. Yet at the beginning and end of the study the relationship was quite strong. See Michael B. Katz, Michael J. Doucet, and Mark J. Stern, *The Social Organization of Early Industrial Capitalism* (Cambridge, Mass., 1982), pp. 336–337.

21. Stewart E. Tolnay, Stephen N. Graham, and Avery M. Guest, "Own-Child Estimates of U.S. White Fertility, 1886–1900," *Historical Methods* 15:3 (Summer 1982), pp. 127–138. The measure of family limitation used by the authors is the "m" developed by Coale and Trussell. See Ansley J. Coale and T. James Trussell, "Model Fertility Schedules: Variations in the Age Structure of Childbearing in Human Populations," *Population Index* 39 (1974), pp. 185–258, and "Technical Note: Finding the Two Parameters That Specify a Model Schedule of Marital Fertility," *Population Index* 44 (1978), pp. 203–213.

22. Tolnay, Graham, and Guest, "Own-Child Estimates," p. 132. In a more recent study, Guest and Tolnay have examined the variations in fertility between cities. They found that the structure of the economy (measured by the proportion of occupations in the textile, primary, or advanced manufacturing sector) and the proportion of foreign-born in the population affected fertility through the intervening influences of women's work and school attendance. While important in establishing the variations across communities, this study demonstrates the difficulty of capturing both the broad national and local contextual influences on fertility. Avery M. Guest and Stewart Tolnay, "Urban Industrial Structure and Fertility: The Case of Large American Cities," *Journal of Interdisciplinary History* 13:3 (Winter 1983), pp. 387–409.

23. Michael Haines, *Fertility and Occupation: Population Patterns in Industrialization* (New York, 1979).

24. Haines, *Fertility and Occupation*, p. 52.

25. Frank W. Notestein, "Economic Problems of Population Change," in *Proceedings of the Eighth International Conference of Agricultural Economists* (London, 1953), quoted in Ansley J. Coale, "The Demographic Transition Reconsidered," *International Union for the Scientific Study of Population* (Liège, 1973).

26. Under the direction of Coale, the participants in the European Fertility Project (EFP) estimated a set of demographic parameters for sub-provincial administrative units throughout Europe. Fertility was indexed to that of the Hutterites (I_f) and was broken into three elements: proportion married (I_m), marital fertility (I_g), and illegitimate fertility (I_h).

The EFP largely confirmed the traditional portrait of rising nuptuality and declining fertility. Its contribution, however, was to document the complexity of the European experience. Knodel, for example, discovered that breast-feeding norms and their impact on birth intervals affected German marital fertility. Other monographs found a wide range of fertility rates before the transition and no uniform timing in the start of the decline—the French were controlling fertility in the eighteenth century while the Germans and Portuguese waited until the end of the nineteenth.

Michael Haines, "Recent Developments in Historical Demography: A Review of the European Fertility Project with some Comparisons from Japan," *Historical Methods Newsletter* 11:4 (1979), p. 169; John E. Knodel, *The Decline of Fertility in Germany, 1871–1939* (Princeton, 1974); Etienne van de Walle, *The Female Population of France in the Nineteenth Century: A Reconstruction of 82 Departements* (Princeton, N.J., 1974).

27. Gary S. Becker, "An Economic Analysis of Fertility," in National Bureau of Economic Research, *Demographic and Economic Change in Developed Countries* (Princeton, N.J., 1960); Gary Becker and H. G. Lewis, "On the Interaction between Quantity and Quality in Children," *Journal of Political Economy* 81:2 (1973), pp. S279–288.

28. Peter H. Lindert, *Fertility and Scarcity in America* (Princeton, N.J., 1978), p. 18.

29. John C. Caldwell, "A Theory of Fertility: From High Plateau to Destabilization," *Population and Development Review* 4:4 (December 1978), pp. 553.

30. John C. Caldwell, "Towards a Restatement of Demographic Transition Theory," in Caldwell, ed., *The Persistence of High Fertility* (Canberra, 1977), p. 83.

31. Caldwell, "Toward a Restatement," p. 84.

32. Caldwell, "Theory of Fertility," pp. 568–569.

33. John C. Caldwell, "Mass Education as a Determinant of the Timing of Fertility Decline," *Population and Development Review* 6:2 (June 1980), p. 234.

34. Caldwell, "Mass Education," p. 234.

35. Katz, Doucet, and Stern, *Social Organization*, pp. 285–348.

36. John Knodel and Etienne van de Walle, "Lessons from the Past: Policy Implications of Historical Fertility Studies," *Population and Development Review* 5:2 (June 1979), pp. 217–245.

37. Norman E. Himes. *Medical History of Contraception* (New York, 1963); Gunner Carlsson, "The Decline of Fertility: Innovation or Adjustment Process," *Population Studies* 20 (1966–67), pp. 149–174; E. A. Wrigley, "Family Limitation in Pre-industrial England," *Economic History Review*, 2nd series, 18 (1966), pp. 82–109.

38. Knodel and van de Walle, "Lessons from the Past."

39. Caldwell, "Theory of Fertility," p. 566.

40. Ron Lesthaeghe, "On the Social Control of Human Reproduction," *Population and Development Review* 6:4 (December 1980), pp. 527–548.

41. Lesthaeghe, "Social Control." In "The Fertility Decline in Western Europe, 1870–1930," Lesthaeghe and Chris Wilson test Lesthaeghe's framework using the European Fertility Project's data for Denmark, Germany, Switzerland, Belgium, and Italy. They discovered that fundamentalist religious movements had a strong impact, slowing the fertility decline. "Reactions to such changes (in the ethical system) may occur in such a way that more fundamentalist views are juxtaposed to secular ones; these divergences have

proved to be closely associated with the acceleration or retardation of marital
fertility transition."

42. This is not to underestimate the strength of the moral campaigns against
birth control and abortion. During the late nineteenth and early twentieth
centuries, a variety of groups campaigned successfully to outlaw abortion
and to restrict the availability of birth control information. Yet, if the fertility
rates are to be believed, these movements closed the barn door after the
horse had left. The decline in native white fertility—"race suicide"—had
already occurred, and the actions of moral coercion failed to reverse this
trend.

If anyone was denied knowledge of contraception by these movements, it
was the working-class immigrants of the early twentieth century. Ironically,
if they had any effect, Comstock and his associates may have increased the
gap between native and foreign fertility that so concerned them.

On the organized birth control movement and its opponents, see David M.
Kennedy, *Birth Control in America: The Career of Margaret Sanger* (New Haven,
Conn., 1970); Linda Gordon, *Woman's Body, Woman's Right: A Social History
of Birth Control in America* (New York, 1976); James Reed, *From Private Vice
to Public Virtue: The Birth Control Movement and American Society Since 1830* (New
York, 1978). On the anti-abortion campaign, see James Mohr, *Abortion in
America* (New York, 1978).

2 Economic and Social Development of Buffalo, 1850–1920

1. In addressing these questions, we shall rely on a variety of sources. The
most important are the industrial censuses of the city, reported in published
volumes between 1860 and 1914. Other statistical information, descriptions
of the economy, and the business press of the city will also provide valuable
clues.

2. All figures expressed in constant dollars are based on 1914 dollars.

3. William Thurstone, ed. *Statistics and Information Relative to the Trade and Commerce of Buffalo* (Buffalo, 1874), p. 119.

4. In 1890, the Census Bureau estimated that one hundred dollars of product
in Buffalo cost $25.48 in wages. This was significantly higher than other
manufacturing centers, including Philadelphia ($23.55), Cleveland ($25.04),
Detroit ($24.45), and Chicago ($18.65). *Census of Manufactures* (Washington,
D.C., 1895).

5. Since the reliability of this index is not self-evident, we should explain its
logic and characteristics, which we derive from Steindl and Kalecki. Our
need to rely on a proxy is a result of the absence of data on depreciation.
The standard production function, however, provides us with a way around
this problem.

$$\text{Capital} + \text{Labor} + \text{Material} + \text{Profit} = \text{Cost}$$

This equation acknowledges that the cost of a product is the sum of four
factors: capital, labor, materials, and profit. If we subtract the cost of materials

from both sides of the equation, the right-hand side becomes value-added (VA), which is the sum of capital, labor, and profit. If this equation is then solved for profit, the result is:

$$1 - \text{Labor/VA} - \text{Capital/VA} = \text{Profit/VA}$$

In other words, holding capital per value added constant, LSVA is the inverse of profit's share of value added. Under these conditions, an increase in LSVA is a decrease in profit.

The assumption that capital's share of value added remains constant is hardly realistic. As an industry becomes more capital intensive, capital's share of value added will increase. Thus, if profits were constant, LSVA would tend to decrease over time. Since we are interested in testing Steindl's hypothesis that profits declined between 1860 and 1920, we can interpret any increase in LSVA as a clear indication of declining profitability. At the same time, a decrease in LSVA does not necessarily imply an increase in profitability.

See Michael Kalecki, *Theory of Economic Dynamics* (London, 1954); Joseph Steindl, *Maturity and Stagnation in American Capitalism* (Oxford, Eng., 1952).

6. Steindl, *Maturity and Stagnation*, p. 166.
7. David Landes, *The Unbound Prometheus: Technological Change and Industrial Development in Western Europe from 1750 to the Present* (Cambridge, Mass., 1972).
8. David Nobel, *America by Design: Science, Technology, and the Rise of Corporate Capitalism* (New York, 1977), pp. 15–16.
9. These data are incomplete because the censuses reported no figures on industries with few establishments, to protect confidentiality. For example, we have no data on the steel industry because the Lackawanna Company dominated this field.
10. Robert Kilduff, "Social Buffalo: A Working Community?" unpublished ms. (n.d.). I would like to thank Mr. Kilduff for making this manuscript available to me.
11. Gareth Stedman Jones, *Outcast London: A Study of the Relationship between Classes in Victorian Society* (Oxford, Eng., 1971).
12. *The Live Wire* (1912), p. 380.
13. Samuel P. Hays, "The Politics of Reform in Municipal Government in the Progressive Era," *Pacific Northwest Quarterly* 55 (October 1964), pp. 157–169.
14. J. J. Henderson, *Annual Statement of the Trade and Commerce of Buffalo* (Buffalo, 1855), p. 31.
15. Quoted in Richard Erlich, "The Development of Buffalo, 1900 to 1967," unpublished ms. (Buffalo: University Archives, 1968), p. 23.
16. *Live Wire* (1912), p. 82.
17. Henderson, *Annual Statement*, p. 14; William Thurstone, *Statement of Trade and Commerce of Buffalo* (Buffalo, 1870), p. 13.
18. *Live Wire* (1914), p. 509.
19. Quoted in Erlich, "Development of Buffalo," p. 23.
20 Erlich, "Development of Buffalo."
21. These figures are based on those household heads who were in classifiable occupations. In 1900 and 1915, relatively few heads were unclassifiable

(9 percent in 1900 and 3 percent in 1915). However, in 1855, because of the absence of occupational data for a large share of the population, the percent unclassifiable was 23 percent. All percentages in the text exclude the unclassifiable in their calculation.

22. Robert Wiebe, *The Search for Order, 1877–1920* (New York, 1967), p. 113.

23. Monte Calvert, *The Mechanical Engineer in America, 1830–1910* (Baltimore, 1967), pp. 277–278.

24. Calvert, *Mechanical Engineer*, pp. 277–278.

25. Harry Braverman, *Labor and Monopoly Capitalism: The Degradation of Work in the Twentieth Century* (New York, 1974), pp. 294–295.

26. Daniel Rodgers, *The Work Ethic in Industrializing America, 1850–1920* (Chicago, 1978); Alan Trachtenberg, *The Incorporation of America: Culture and Society in the Gilded Age* (New York, 1982).

27. Katz, Doucet, and Stern, *Social Organization;* Clyde and Sally Griffen, *Natives and Newcomers: The Ordering of Opportunity in Mid-Nineteenth Century Poughkeepsie* (Cambridge, 1978).

28. Suzanne G. Schnittman, "Irregular Employment in Buffalo, New York, from 1870 to 1971," Master's thesis (State University of New York-Brockport, 1979); See also Alexander Keyssar, *Out of Work: The First Century of Unemployment in Massachusetts* (Cambridge, Mass., 1986).

29. Sidney Levy, "The Grain Scoopers of Buffalo: An Essay in Local Labor History," Master's thesis (University of Buffalo, 1940). This sector of the labor market, which included some of the construction trades as well, fits Edwards's description of the subordinate primary sector. While low in skill, they achieved regular employment. Yet the split that Edwards makes between the independent (high-skill, regular employment) and subordinate (low-skill, regular employment) primary sector was not sufficiently widespread before the 1930s to justify making the distinction here. See Richard Edwards, *Contested Terrain: The Transformation of the Workplace in the Twentieth Century* (New York, 1979).

30. Oscar Ornati, *Poverty Amid Affluence* (New York, 1966). These data come from the Bureau of Labor Statistics 1918 cost-of-living survey and cover only native workers. This survey provided detailed data on the income and expenditures of the family during the year. The manuscripts of the survey, housed in the National Archives, were coded and analysed for Buffalo. For more detail on the methodology and findings, see Mark J. Stern, "Demography of Capitalism: Industry, Class, and Fertility in Erie County, New York, 1855–1915," (unpublished Ph.D. dissertation, York University, 1979) Chapter Six.

31. Robert and Helen Lynd, *Middletown: A Study of Modern American Culture* (New York, 1929), p. 161.

32. All names used in the text are fictitious.

33. Tamara K. Hareven, *Family Time and Industrial Time* (New York, 1982); Thomas Dublin, *Women at Work* (New York, 1979); Daniel J. Walkowitz, *Worker City, Company Town: Iron and Cotton Worker Protest in Troy and Cohoes, New York 1855–84* (Urbana, 1978).

34. Louise A. Tilly and Joan W. Scott, *Women, Work, and Family* (New York, 1978).

3   Differential Fertility in Erie County

1. Clifford Geertz, "Ritual and Social Change: A Javanese Example" in *The Interpretation of Culture* (New York, 1973), pp. 142–169.
2. The data for this study come from three samples drawn from the Federal Census of 1900 and the New York state censuses of 1855 and 1915. For 1855, the sample included the entire population of the city of Buffalo and a 20 percent sample of households from rural Erie County. For 1900, a 7 percent sample of the County, stratified by ethnicity, was drawn, while in 1915, the sampling fraction was 10 percent. The twentieth century samples were disproportionate, with ethnic groups (Germans and Canadians in 1900, Germans, Poles, Austro-Hungarians, Italians, and Russians in 1915) being oversampled. For more details on the sampling scheme and the characteristics of the sample, see Stern, "The Demography of Capitalism."
3. On the "own-children" method, see Donald J. Bogue, *Demographic Techniques of Fertility Analysis* (Chicago, 1971) and Lee-Jay Cho, W. H. Grabill, and Donald J. Bogue, *Differential Current Fertility in the United States* (Chicago, 1970). The method has also been used by Haines, *Fertility and Occupation*, and Hareven and Vinovskis, "Marital Fertility, Ethnicity, and Occupation," and "Patterns of Childbearing."

I have followed Hareven and Vinovskis in age-standardizing the fertility ratio. The age-specific ratio for each five-year cohort was multiplied by a standard set of decimals (0.10, 0.17, 0.21, 0.22, 0.17, and 0.13). Unless otherwise noted, all ratios in the text and tables are age-standardized. When comparisons are made across years, the ratios have been corrected for mortality. For 1855, I used a set of life tables for urban, rural, native, and foreign-born populations developed by Haines for New York State based on the 1865 state census. For 1900 and 1915, I used the Brass-Sullivan-Trussel technique for estimating child mortality from data on children-ever-born and children-surviving in 1900. These estimates were then fitted to model life tables (Coale and Demeny West). For more detail on the methods, see Stern, "Demography of Capitalism." See also W. Brass, *Methods for Estimating Fertility and Mortality from Limited and Defective Data* (Chapel Hill, N.C., 1975); J. M. Sullivan, "Models for the Estimation of the Probability of Dying between Birth and Exact Ages in Early Childhood," *Population Studies* 26:1 (April 1972), pp. 79–97; T. J. Trussel, "A Re-estimation of the Multiplying Factors for the Brass Technique for Determining Childhood Survivorship Rates," *Population Studies* 29:1 (April 1975), pp. 97–107; A. J. Coale and P. Demeny, *Regional Model Life Tables and Stable Populations* (Princeton, N.J., 1966).

4. Anthony Giddens, *The Class Structure of Advanced Societies* (London, 1973), p. 106. Recently, David Hogan has differentiated "categorical" conceptions of class from an "historical" conception, arguing that the former is "not intrinsically historical." David John Hogan, *Class and Reform: School and Society in Chicago, 1880–1930* (Philadelphia, 1985), p. xiv.

5. Katz, Doucet and Stern, *Social Organization*, p. 62.

6. For each census, every household head with a artisanal occupational title was checked against the business directories of the city. If a positive identification was made, the case's occupational classification was made "masters and manufacturer" rather than "skilled worker." The records were linked for both name and address. If the link was ambiguous, the occupation was not changed. Since only one in ten skilled workers was a master artisan, an incorrect classification would have less of an impact on this group than on the other. For more detailed information on this procedure, see Stern, "The Demography of Capitalism."

7. While this set of categories is used for all census years, one important change was made. The progenitor of the business employee was the clerk, the "man Friday" of the nineteenth-century enterprise. As we have noted, the clerks had little to do with the business employees of the early twentieth century; it makes sense to see the clerks of 1855 as part of the old business class and the newer business employees as part of the new business class. Therefore, when we use this division, we include the clerks with the old business stratum.

8. The one group that would have been important to differentiate is factory workers. However, the census makes it difficult to distinguish this group from skilled workers in non-factory settings. Therefore, we have included them both in the skilled worker group.

9. These data and those presented below are laid out in considerably more detail in my dissertation, "The Demography of Capitalism."

10. For each group, a regression equation was estimated with children-ever-born as the dependent variable and with age (log transformation) and age-at-marriage as the independent variables. This equation, then, is the best estimate of the trend of children-ever-born using data on women of all ages. These equations were then used to compute completed fertility by substituting the age of 50 and the age-at-marriage of 23 for the independent variables. Since the relationship of age and fertility may not fit the logarithmic curve perfectly, the estimates of completed fertility should not be taken as absolute, but used for relative comparisons across groups. For more detailed description of these methods, see Stern, "Demography of Capitalism."

11. The modification that was required was necessitated by the prevalence of multiple-family dwelling in Buffalo. Since each family in a building was credited with the full value of the building, this value had to be apportioned among the various families. Our measure, dwelling value per capita, divided the dwelling value by the size of each family in it. For example, in a two-family building worth $5,000 with two families—one of six and the other of four members—the first family's dwelling value per capita would be $3,000, and the second family's, $2,000.

For a fuller description of this variable and its relationship to other economic variables, see Katz, Doucet, and Stern, *Social Organization*, p. 407.

12. In this analysis, the new business class was excluded because 86 percent of the families in this group were in the top forty percent of the economic order.

13. On natural fertility, see J. Bourgeois-Pichat, "Social and Biological Determinants of Human Fertility in Non-Industrial Societies," *Proceedings of the American Philosophical Society* 111:3 (1967), pp. 160–163; Geoffrey Hawthorn, *The Sociology of Fertility* (London, 1970), pp. 10–14, 120–125.

14. "It is important to note that family limitation is not synonymous with 'birth control.' Family limitation depends on the number of children already born and refers specifically to behavior designed to stop childbearing altogether. The term birth control, on the other hand, encompasses both behavior intended to stop births and deliberate attempts to space births. . . . Birth spacing is not inconsistent with family limitation. However, situations where couples deliberately attempt to space births but are unconcerned with the ultimate number . . . are classified as natural fertility rather than family limitation." Etienne van de Walle and John Knodel, "Europe's Fertility Transition: New Evidence and Lessons for Today's Developing World," *Population Bulletin* 34:6 (February 1980), p. 10.

15. A. J. Coale and T. J. Trussel, "Model Fertility Schedules: Variation in the Age Structure of Childbearing in Human Populations," *Population Index* 40:2 (April 1974), pp. 185–258. The ratios used in the present study are different from the probabilities of bearing a child, which are the basis of the "m." This difference is particularly important for younger women since they are less likely to have been married for the entire five years preceding the census. For this reason, we have concentrated on the age-specific fertility of older married women.

16. One caution is in order. We are attempting to identify the shift in patterns of fertility between age cohorts. To do so, ideally we would need longitudinal data on individual cohorts through time. Our "snapshot" data combine the experience of several cohorts and thus pose the possibility that one could incorrectly infer cohort patterns from cross-sectional data.

17. Van de Walle and Knodel, "Europe's Fertility Transition," p. 32. On the demographic history of Ireland, see Oliver MacDonagh, "The Irish Famine Emigration to the United States," *Perspectives in American History* 10 (1976), pp. 357–448. While the Irish data suggest the absence of family limitation, there are a number of possibilities that could account for the observed pattern, including absence of husband and impaired fecundity. In my view, however, conscious child spacing appears to be the most plausible of these alternatives. I would like to thank an anonymous reviewer for SUNY Press for pointing out these alternatives.

18. The case for knowledge of fertility control before the transition is also supported by data on age at marriage and fertility. Among women in their thirties, those who had married late had significantly higher fertility than women who had married earlier. While other explanations are possible, this seems to suggest that those who married early were somehow limiting their

fertility. Whether this was inadvertant—the result perhaps of reduced coital frequency—or conscious is difficult to determine. For a discussion of these data, see Michael B. Katz and Mark J. Stern, "Fertility, Class, and Industrial Capitalism: Erie County, New York, 1855–1915," *American Quarterly* 33:1 (Spring 1981), pp. 63–92.

19. Geertz, "Ritual and Social Change," p. 144.

20. Joseph Schumpeter, *Capitalism, Socialism, and Democracy* (New York, 1950), p. 160.

21. Joseph Kett, *Rites of Passage: Adolescence in America: 1790 to the Present* (New York, 1977), pp. 151–152.

22. Rodgers, *Work Ethic*, pp. 105–106.

23. Robert and Helen Lynd, *Middletown*, p. 46, passim.

24. Rodgers, *Work Ethic*.

25. J. A. Banks, *Prosperity and Parenthood: A Study of Family Planning among the Victorian Middle Classes* (London, 1954). For further development of his theory, see J. A. and Olive Banks, *Feminism and Family Planning in Victorian England* (New York, 1964) and J. A. Banks, *Victorian Values: Secularism and the Size of Families* (London, 1981). For a criticism of Banks's argument, see Patricia Branca, *Silent Sisterhood: Middle Class Women in the Victorian Home* (London, 1976).

26. Tilly and Scott, *Women, Work, and Family*; Katz, Doucet, and Stern, *Social Organization*, pp. 285–347; John Modell, Frank F. Furstenberg, and Theodore Hershberg, "Social Change and Transitions to Adulthood in Historical Perspective," in Theodore Hershberg, ed., *Philadelphia: Work, Space, Family, and Group Experience in the 19th Century* (New York, 1981), pp. 311–342; John Modell and Tamara K. Hareven, "Urbanization and the Malleable Household: An Examination of Boarding and Lodging in American Families," *Journal of Marriage and the Family* 35 (August 1973), pp. 467–478; Hogan, *Class and Reform*, pp. 96–137.

27. Steven Dubnoff, "The Life-Cycle and Economic Welfare: Historical Change in the Economic Constraints on Working Class Family Life, 1860–1974." Unpublished ms.

28. In relating economic conditions and subjective orientation, two elements must be separated. From an *economic* perspective, the lack of predictability means that the "costs" of planning outweigh its benefits. Therefore, it is rational for an actor not to plan in this situation. *Psychologically*, unpredictability may foster feelings of impotence. The argument obviously hinges on whether the psychological elements are so harmful that the actor becomes unable to respond when actual conditions do change. For a discussion of the issue, see Glen H. Elder, Jr. "Approaches to Social Change and the Family," in John Demos and Sarane Spence Boocock, eds., *Turning Points: Historical and Sociological Essays on the Family* (Chicago, 1978), pp. S1–38.

29. Stephen Meyer III, *The Five Dollar Day: Labor Management and Social Control in the Ford Motor Company, 1908–1921* (Albany, N.Y., 1981); James Green, *The World of the Worker: Labor in Twentieth Century America* (New York, 1980), pp. 103–111; Peter R. Shergold, *Working-Class Life: The "American Standard"*

in Comparative Perspective, 1899–1913 (Pittsburgh, 1982). Through an analysis of specific trades in Pittsburgh and Birmingham, Shergold demonstrates the ideological character of the "American Standard." Yet, in doing so, he may underestimate the changes that were experienced by American workers compared to their European counterparts and the impact these had on their lives.

30. Gareth Stedman Jones, "Working Class Culture and Working Class Politics in London, 1870–1900: Notes on the Remaking of a Working Class," *Journal of Social History* 7:4 (Summer 1974), pp. 498–499. Whereas the English working class, still mired in poverty, retained more interest in a collective culture—the music hall, pub, and sidewalk sociability—in the United States, the upper tier of the working class made a different, more private accommodation with the social order.

31. Katz, Doucet, and Stern, *Social Organization*, ch. 9; Michael Anderson, *Family Structure in Nineteenth Century Lancashire* (Cambridge, Eng., 1971); Modell and Hareven, "The Malleable Household."

32. Clyde and Sally Griffen, *Natives and Newcomers*, pp. 207–227.

33. Michael B. Katz and Ian E. Davey, "Youth and Early Industrialization in a Canadian City," in Demos and Boocock, *Turning Points*, pp. S81–119.

34. Paul Osterman, *Getting Started: The Youth Labor Market* (Cambridge, Mass, 1980); Floyd Musgrove, *Youth and the Social Order* (Bloomington, Ind., 1964), pp. 73–74. For a discussion of supply and demand factors in child labor, see Hogan, *Class and Reform*, pp. 55–57.

35. Braverman, *Labor and Monopoly Capitalism*, p. 379.

36. Jane Synge, "The Transition from School to Work: Working Class Adolescence in Early 20th Century Hamilton." Paper presented at York University, 1977; C. Wright Mills, *White Collar: The American Middle Classes* (New York, 1951), pp. 246–250, passim.

37. Trachtenberg, *Incorporation of America*; Edward Shorter, *The Making of the Modern Family*, p. 14, passim., argues that America was "born modern" and, therefore, did not experience as dramatic of a change in culture as Europe did. While this may gloss over some fairly important transformations, it is true that the fertility decline in the United States was well underway by 1855 and that the native population's decline in fertility was probably influenced more by structural than cultural changes.

38. See Hubert M. Blalock, Jr., *Social Statistics*, Second Edition (New York, 1972), pp. 230, 456–57, for a discussion of interaction and multicolinearity. If there is no interaction between two variables, they have *additive* influences on a third variable. See also Katz and Stern, "Fertility, Class, and Industrial Capitalism," p. 78.

39. This conclusion is reinforced by multivariate analysis, as well. If we control statistically for other variables, both social class and ethnicity retain significant relationships with fertility. For example, in 1900, the fertility ratios of the various occupational groups, controlling for other factors, were 766 per thousand for the old business class, 731 for the new business class, 856 for skilled workers, and 934 for unskilled workers. The sharpness of these differentials was reduced by multivariate analysis, but it remained clear and significant. For a more detailed presentation of these data, see Stern, "Demography of Capitalism," chs. 3, 4, and 5.

40. This analysis is complicated by the difference in the migration variable on each of the censuses. The variable on the 1855 census measures length of residence in the city and town. This variable is recorded for the entire population. In 1900 and 1915, the variable is length of residence in the United States, which obviously is only recorded for the foreign-born.

41. See Katz, Doucet, and Stern, *Social Organization*, pp. 113–130 on transiency in Erie County. On persistence in 19th-century North America, see Stephan Thernstrom and Peter R. Knights, "Men in Motion: Some Data and Speculations about Urban Population Mobility in Nineteenth-Century America," *Journal of Interdisciplinary History* 1 (1970), pp. 18–19. Thernstrom reviews a number of persistence studies in his *The Other Bostonians: Poverty and Progress in the American Metropolis* (Cambridge, Mass., 1973).

42. Katz, Doucet, and Stern, *Social Organization*, pp. 133–148.

43. Katz, Doucet, and Stern, *Social Organization*, p. 130. See also Michael B. Katz, *The People of Hamilton*. In Buffalo, a few statistics give the flavor of the pervasiveness of migration. Among men 25–54 years of age, New Englanders had lived in the city for an average of 10 years, compared to 8 and 6.5 years for Irish and Germans. Among occupational groups, the length of residence of upper-class proprietors was actually lower than among laborers for all ethnic groups.

44. Harry Jerome, *Migration and the Business Cycle* (New York: National Bureau for Economic Research, 1926), pp. 44–45, passim., cited in Gabriel Kolko, *Main Currents in Modern American History* (New York, 1976), p. 70; Michael J. Piore, *Birds of Passage: Migrant Labor and Industrial Societies* (New York, 1979), pp. 141–166. According to Jerome, 52 percent of "Russians" returned, but this does not include the "Hebrew" population, whose rate was the lowest of any group.

45. Kolko, *Main Currents*, p. 71.

4   Schooling and Fertility in Erie County

1. Judith Blake, "Are Babies Consumer Durables?: A Critique of the Economic Theory of Reproductive Motivation," *Population Studies* 22 (1968), p. 15.

2. Caldwell, "A Theory of Fertility," p. 568.

3. Caldwell, "Mass Education," pp. 225–255.

4. Caldwell, "Mass Education," pp. 229–236.

5. Caldwell cites approvingly a report from Mexico: "Going to school has . . . awakened new desires in children by removing them from the limited sphere of parental influence. They are no longer content to stay within patio walls at the beck and call of their mother." "Mass Education," p. 243.

6. Virginia Yans-McLaughin, *Family and Community: Italian Immigrants in Buffalo, 1880–1930* (Ithaca, N.Y., 1977).
7. On Elwood Cubberley, see David K. Cohen and Marvin Lazerson, "Education and the Corporate Order," in Michael B. Katz, ed., *Education in American History: Readings on the Social Issues* (New York, 1973), pp. 321–323; Lawrence Cremin, *The Transformation of the School: Progressivism in American Education* (New York, 1961).
8. Michael B. Katz, *The Irony of Early School Reform* (Cambridge, Mass., 1967); Katz, "The Fate of Educational Reform," in Katz, ed., *Education in American History*, p. 301. Other revisionist studies include Clarence Karier, *Shaping the American Educational State* (New York, 1973); Marvin Lazerson, *Origins of the Urban School* (Cambridge, Mass., 1971); Samuel Bowles and Herbert Gintis, *Schooling in Capitalist America* (New York, 1976).
9. Diane Ravitch, *Revisionists Revised: A Critique of the Radical Attack on the Schools* (New York, 1978); Katz, "The Origins of Public Education: A Reassessment," *History of Education Quarterly* 16:1 (Winter 1976), pp. 399–400. For a criticism of the "social control" perspective, see Hogan, *Class and Reform*, p. xii, passim. T. Jackson Lear has discussed the wider implications of the concept of cultural hegemony in his "The Concept of Cultural Hegemony: Problems and Possibilities," *American Historical Review* 90:3 (June 1985), pp. 567–593.
10. David Hogan, "Education and the Making of the Chicago Working Class." *History of Education Quarterly* 18:3 (Fall 1978), pp. 227–270.
11. Hogan, "Chicago," p. 245.
12. Miriam Cohen, "Italian-American Women in New York City, 1900–1950," in Milton Cantor and Bruce Laurie, eds., *Class, Sex, and the Woman Worker* (Westport, Conn., 1977), pp. 120–121.
13. Cohen, "Italian-American Women," p. 135. See also Cohen, "Changing Educational Strategies among Immigrant Generations: New York Italians in Comparative Perspective," *Journal of Social History* 15:3 (Spring 1984), pp. 443–466.
14. A. J. Perlmann, "Education and the Social Structure of an American City," Ph.D. dissertation (Harvard University, 1980).
15. Perlmann, "Education," 2, p. 69.
16. On increase in college attendance, see Paula Fass, *The Damned and the Beautiful: American Youth in the 1920s* (New York, 1977), pp. 60, 84–85.
17. This measure does not allow us to measure the intensity of school attendance, but the census is not an appropriate source for investigating this question. This measure is sensitive, however, to changes among older teenagers, the group most affected by the labor market changes of the late 19th and early 20th centuries.
18. Among the daughters of the business class, changes between 1900 and 1915 were not notable. Business employees' daughters had the highest rate of school attendance in both years. In 1900 rates among the business class ranged from 34 percent for agents, merchants, masters, and manufacturers to 61 percent for business employees. In 1915, the lowest rate belonged to

masters and manufacturers (36 percent) and the highest again to business employees (56 percent).

19. Katz and Davey, "Youth and Early Industrialization."

20. On the changing job market, see Paul Osterman, *Getting Started: The Youth Labor Market* (Cambridge, Mass., 1980), pp. 51–62. On the "child-centered school," see Richard Hofstadter, *Anti-Intellectualism in American Life* (New York, 1962), and Hogan, *Class and Reform*, pp. 82–93. On vocationalism, see Harvey Kantor and David B. Tyack, eds., *Work, Youth, and Schooling: Historical Perspectives on Vocationalism in American Education* (Stanford, Ca., 1982), especially the contributions of Grubb and Lazerson, Kett, and Hogan.

21. On the relative position of the Irish and Germans at midcentury see Katz, Doucet, and Stern, *Social Organization*, pp. 89–97.

22. On labor recruitment and education, see David Hogan, "Making It in America: Work, Education, and Social Structure," in Kantor and Tyack, *Work, Youth, and Schooling*, pp. 159–160. On changes in industrial recruitment and control, see Richard C. Edwards, *Contested Terrain: The Transformation of the Workplace in America* (New York, 1979), ch. 4.

23. Maxine S. Sellers, *Ethnic Communities and Education in Buffalo, New York: Politics, Power, and Group Identity, 1830–1979* (Buffalo, 1979), pp. 14–24.

24. Yans-McLaughlin, "Patterns of Work and Family Organization: Buffalo's Italians," in T. K. Rabb and R. I. Rotberg, eds., *The Family in History: Interdisciplinary Essays* (New York, 1971), p. 117, and *Family and Community*; Cohen, "Italian-American Women."

25. Yans-McLaughlin, "Italian Women and Work: Experience and Perception," in Cantor and Laurie, *Class, Sex, and the Woman Worker*, p. 103; Louise Tilly, "Comments on Yans-McLaughlin and Davidoff Papers," *Journal of Social History* 5 (Summer 1974), pp. 452–459.

26. However, these data do qualify Hogan's belief that immigrant attitudes appear to have given way to a homogeneous "instrumental" attitude toward education. The Erie County data suggest that this process of cultural innovation occurred only among boys. For girls, the strength of cultural influences continued. The role of education in the "making" of the working-class was a male-only affair.

27. Again, it is important to emphasize that Caldwell is primarily concerned with the spread of mass education, not its extension into adolescence. Still, particularly in the case of the new immigrants, the impact of education on traditional peasant culture seems to be a test of his hypothesis.

28. The fertility measure used here is the same as in Chapter Three: the estimated children ever born, based on a regression of children ever born by the natural logarithm of the women's ages. The actual levels should not be taken literally, since the logarithm overestimates fertility in women's later years. Rather the meaningful data are the comparisons between groups.

29. Those families with no older teenagers were excluded from this analysis. In addition, families with *some* of their children in high school and some not were excluded. This included only seven and nine percent of the sample in the case of boys and girls, respectively.

30. The beta weights were .35 for boys' attendance and .09 for girls'.

31. The beta-weight for fertility and a combination of schooling and social strata was significant at the .001 level for boys' secondary schooling and at greater than the .05 level for girls' schooling.

5 Rural Fertility in Erie County

1. Richard Hofstadter, *The Age of Reform: From Bryan to FDR* (New York, 1955); Lawrence Goodwin, *Democratic Promise: The Populist Moment in America* (New York, 1976); William Leuchtenberg, *The Perils of Prosperity, 1914–1932* (Chicago, 1958), pp. 204–225. This chapter appeared in a different form in the *Journal of Social History* 16:4 (Summer 1983), pp. 49–64.

2. For a discussion of the American historical demographic literature, see Chapter 1 above.

3. Wendell Bash, "Differential Fertility in Madison County, New York, 1865," *The Milbank Memorial Fund Quarterly* 33 (1955), pp. 161–186.

4. See Katz, Doucet, and Stern, *Social Organization*, p. 9; J. H. French, *Gazatteer of the State of New York* (Syracuse, 1860), pp. 279–294.

5. Paul W. Gates, *The Farmer's Age: Agriculture, 1815–1860* (New York, 1960).

6. Easterlin, Alter, and Condran, "Farm and Farm Families," pp. 54–57.

7. Hofstadter, *Age of Reform*, pp. 23–93, provides one image of the "folklore" of Populism, while Goodwin, *Democratic Promise*, gives a more sympathetic version and links it to the social and economic realities that the farmers confronted.

8. C. H. Danhof, *Change in Agriculture: The Northern United States, 1820–1870* (Cambridge, Mass., 1969), pp. 88–98; Gates, *Farmers' Age*, pp. 36–39.

9. Gates, *Farmers' Age*, p. 33.

10. Ibid., p. 39; P. W. Bidwell and J. I. Falconer, *History of Agriculture in the Northern United States 1620–1860* (New York, 1941), p. 449. Note that there was a considerable amount of tenancy in the antebellum North.

11. U. P. Hendrick. *A History of Agriculture in the State of New York* (New York, 1966 [1933]), p. 353.

12. Hofstadter, *Age of Reform*, and Goodwin, *Democratic Promise*, provide the entrepreneurial and yeoman interpretations of Populism. Gabriel Kolko, *Main Currents in Modern American History*, pp. 25–29, uses a peasant model.

13. Katz, Doucet, and Stern, *Social Organization*, ch. 4.

14. See Anthony Giddens, *The Class Structure of the Advanced Societies* (London, 1973), pp. 99–112, on "class structuration."

15. J. Hajnal, "European Marriage Patterns in Perspective," in David V. Glass and D. E. C. Eversley, eds., *Population in History: Essays in Historical Demography* (London, 1965), pp. 101–146; van de Walle and Knodel, "Europe's Fertility Transition," pp. 10–15.

16. Jerome Blum, *The End of the Old Order in Rural Europe* (Princeton, N.J., 1978), p. 105.

17. For a more detailed presentation of these data, see Stern, "Demography of Capitalism."
18. Charles Tilly, "The Historical Study of Vital Processes," in Tilly, ed. *Historical Studies in Changing Fertility*, pp. 32–34.
19. On rural depopulation, see Harold Seth Barron, "Their Town: Economy and Society in a Settled Rural Community: Chelsea, Vermont, 1840–1900," Ph.D. dissertation (University of Pennsylvania, 1980).

6 Fertility and Social History

1. Anthony Giddens, *The Constitution of Society: An Outline of the Theory of Structuration* (Berkeley and Los Angeles, 1984).
2. Katz, Doucet, and Stern, *Social Organization*, p. 25. Some recent critical discussion includes, Stuart Blumin, "The Hypothesis of Middle-Class Formation in Nineteenth-Century America: A Critique and Some Proposals," *American Historical Review* 90:2 (April 1985), p. 310, passim.; and Fred Matthews, " 'Hobbesian Populism': Interpretive Paradigms and Moral Vision in American Historiography," *Journal of American History* 72:1 (June 1985), pp. 113–114.
3. Katz, Doucet, and Stern, *Social Organization*, p. 392.
4. Giddens, *Class Structure of Advanced Societies*, p. 110.
5. Wiebe, *Search for Order*.
6. Stedman Jones, "Working Class Culture"; see also Hogan, *Class and Reform*, pp. 136–37.
7. The outstanding account of the impact of improved standards of living on the breakdown of working-class association is Michael Young and Peter Wilmott, *Family and Kinship in East London* (Hammondsworth, Eng., 1962). They link the move of families to suburban housing estates with the increased nuclearizing of the family: "The 'home' and the family of marriage becomes the focus of a man's life, as of his wife's, far more completely than in the East End. 'You lose contact with parents and relations once you move out here,' said Mr. Curtis. 'You seem to centre yourself more on the home. Everybody lives in a little world of their own.' " (p. 145). Herbert Gans, *The Urban Villagers: Group and Class in the Life of Italian-Americans* (New York, 1962) reaches similar conclusions about the resettlement of the residents of Boston's West End.
8. For better or worse, the vast literature spawned by the "culture of poverty" debate of the 1960s brought a fresh appreciation of the role of gift giving and exchange among the poor. See, in particular, Carol Stack, *All Our Kin: Strategies for Survival in a Black Community* (New York, 1974), pp. 32–43.
9. T. J. Jackson Lear, "The Concept of Cultural Hegemony: Problems and Possibilities," *American Historical Review* 90:3 (June 1985), pp. 568, 574.
10. Ernest W. Burgess, Harvey J. Locke, and Mary Margaret Thomes, *The Family: From Tradition to Companionship* (New York, 1971), quoted in Glen

Elder, *Children of the Great Depression: Social Change in Life Experience* (Chicago, 1974), p. 286.

11. Giddens, *Constitution of Society*, p. 236.

12. Thomas Kuhn, *The Structure of Scientific Revolutions*, 2nd ed. (Chicago, 1970).

13. Anthony F. C. Wallace, "Appendix: Paradigmatic Processes in Cultural Change," in his *Rockdale*, pp. 477–486; Glen H. Elder, Jr., "Approaches to Social Change and the Family," in Demos and Boocock, *Turning Points*, pp. S1–38.

14. Elder, "Social Change and the Family," p. 18.

15. Elder, "Social Change and the Family," p. 18.

16. Elder, *Children of the Great Depression*, p. 12. While I find Elder's formulation of family and social change to be the best in the literature, I do take issue with some elements of it. In particular, his use of "adaptation" allows evolutionary imagery to enter his conceptualization by the back door. See Giddens, *Constitution of Society*, p. 233–236, on the concept of adaptation.

17. Anthony Giddens, *Central Problems in Social Theory: Action, Structure and Contradiction in Social Analysis* (Berkeley and Los Angeles, 1979), pp. 123–128.

18. Oscar Handlin, *The Uprooted* (New York, 1951), p. 239.

19. Yans-McLaughlin, *Family and Community*; Herbert Gutman, *Society and Culture in Industrializing America* (New York, 1977); Kolko, *Main Currents in Modern American History*, pp. 94–99.

20. This underlines as well the cultural content of family strategy. The family strategy of the working class was not "automatic" nor "self-evident": it was a set of rules and resources that had developed over time. Treating it only as either a structural response or a psychological condition misses the dynamic quality of social "structuration." Finally, it is worth noting that the one element of the old working-class strategy that did not recur was the large family. Fertility reached an all-time low during the 1930s. Thus, once adopted, the small family was not easily abandoned.

21. Elder, *Children of the Great Depression*, p. 287; Elder has discussed the impact of the Depression experience on post-war fertility in his "Scarcity and Prosperity in Post-War Childbearing: Explanations from a Life-Course Perspective," in Michael Gordon, ed. *The American Family in Socio-Historical Perspective*, 3rd ed. (New York, 1982), pp. 182–208.

22. Barbara Ehrenreich, *The Hearts of Men: American Dreams and the Flight from Commitment* (Garden City, New York, 1984). One issue that this study cannot adequately address is the change in the cultural role of children discussed by Viviana Zelizer in her important new book. According to Zelizer, between 1870 and 1930 the value of children went through a profound social change, from economically valuable to worthless but "priceless." Focusing on the "independent effects of cultural factors," Zelizer contends that by the 1930s, the child had been "sacralized," that is, invested with a sentimental or religious meaning. See Viviana A. Zelizer, *Pricing the Priceless Child: The Changing Social Value of Children* (New York, 1985).

23. Christopher Lasch, *Haven in a Heartless World: The Family Besieged* (New York, 1977).

Bibliography

Anderson, Michael. *Family Structure in Nineteenth Century Lancashire.* New York: Cambridge University Press, 1971.

Banks, Joseph A. *Prosperity and Parenthood: A Study of Family Planning among the Victorian Middle Classes.* London: Routledge and Kegan Paul, 1954.

————. *Victorian Values: Secularism and the Size of Families.* London: Routledge and Kegan Paul, 1981.

———— and Olive Banks. *Feminism and Family Planning in Victorian England.* New York: Schocken Books, 1964.

Barron, Harold Seth. "Their Town: Economy and Society in a Settled Rural Community: Chelsea, Vermont, 1840–1900." Unpublished Ph.D. dissertation, University of Pennsylvania, 1980.

Bash, Wendell H. "Differential Fertility in Madison County, New York, 1865," *Milbank Memorial Fund Quarterly* 33 (1955): 161–186.

————. "Changing Birth Rates in Developing America: New York State, 1840–1875," *Milbank Memorial Fund Quarterly* 41 (April 1963): 161–182.

Becker, Gary. "An Economic Analysis of Fertility." In *Demographic Change in Developed Countries,* edited by National Bureau of Economic Research, Princeton, N.J.: Princeton University Press, 1960.

———— and H. G. Lewis. "On the Interaction Between Quantity and Quality of Children," *Journal of Political Economy* 81:2 (1973): S279–288.

Bidwell, P. W. and J. I. Falconer. *History of Agriculture in the Northern United States, 1620–1860.* New York: P. Smith, 1941.

Blake, Judith. "Are Babies Consumer Durables: A Critique in of the Economic Theory of Reproductive Motivation," *Population Studies* 22 (1968): 5–25.

Blalock, H. M. *Social Statistics.* 2nd edition. New York: McGraw-Hill, 1972.

Blum, Jerome. *The End of the Old Order in Rural Europe.* Princeton, N.J.: Princeton University Press, 1978.

Blumin, Stuart. "The Hypothesis of Middle-Class Formation in Nineteenth-Century America: A Critique and Some Proposals," *American Historical Review* 90:2 (April 1985): 299–339.

Bogue, Donald J. *Demographic Techniques of Fertility Analysis*. Chicago: Community and Family Study Center, 1971.

Bourgeois-Pichat, J. "Social and Biological Determinants of Human Fertility in Non-Industrial Societies," *Proceedings of the American Philosophical Society* 111:3 (1967): 160–163.

Bowles, Samuel and Herbert Gintis. *Schooling in Capitalist America*. New York: Basic Books, 1976.

Branca, Patricia. *Silent Sisterhood: Middle-Class Women in the Victorian Home*. London: Croom Helm, 1976.

Brass, W. *Methods for Estimating Fertility and Mortality from Limited and Defective Data*. Chapel Hill: University of North Carolina Press, 1975.

Braverman, Harry. *Labor and Monopoly Capitalism: The Degradation of Work in the Twentieth Century*. New York and London: Monthly Review Press, 1974.

Brody, David. *Steelworkers in America: The Non-Union Era*. Cambridge, Mass.: Harvard University Press, 1960.

Brody, D. S. "Consumption and the Style of Life." In Lance E. Davis *et al. American Economic Growth: An Economist's History of the United States*. New York: Harper and Row, 1972.

Buffalo Chamber of Commerce. *The Live Wire*, vols. 3–5 (1911–1914).

Caldwell, John C. "Toward a Restatement of Demographic Transition Theory." In *The Persistence of High Fertility*, edited by John Caldwell. Canberra: Australian National University, 1977.

———. "A Theory of Fertility: From High Plateau to Destabilization," *Population and Development Review* 4:4 (December 1978): 553–578.

———. "Mass Education as a Determinant of the Timing of Fertility Decline," *Population and Development Review* 6:2 (June 1980): 225–255.

——— and L. Ruzicka. "The Australian Fertility Transition: An Analysis," *Population and Development Review* 4:1 (March 1978): 81–103.

Calvert, Monte. *The Mechanical Engineer in America, 1830–1910*. Baltimore: Johns Hopkins University Press, 1967.

Carlsson, Gunner. "The Decline of Fertility: Innovation or Adjustment Process," *Population Studies* 20 (1966–67): 149–174.

Chandler, Alfred D., Jr. *The Visible Hand: The Managerial Revolution in American Business*. Cambridge, Mass.: The Belknap Press, 1977.

Cho, Lee-Jay, W. H. Grabill, and Donald J. Bogue. *Differential Current Fertility in the United States*. Chicago: Community and Family Study Center, 1970.

Coale, Ansley J. "The Demographic Transition Reconsidered." Liege: International Union for the Scientific Study of Population, 1973.

——— and Paul Demeny. *Regional Model Life Tables and Stable Populations*. Princeton, N.J.: Princeton University Press, 1966.

——— and T. J. Trussell. "Model Fertility Schedules: Variations in the Age Structure of Childbearing in Human Populations," *Population Index* 39 (1974): 185–258.

————. "Technical Note: Finding the Two Parameters That Specify a Model Schedule of Marital Fertility," *Population Index* 44 (1978): 203–213.

———— and Marvin Zelnick. *New Estimates of Fertility and Population in the United States.* Princeton, N.J.: Princeton University Press, 1963.

Cohen, David and Marvin Lazerson. "Education and the Corporate Order." In *Education and American History: Readings on the Social Issues,* edited by Michael B. Katz. New York: Praeger, 1973.

Cohen, Mariam. "Italian-America Women in New York City, 1900–1950." In *Class, Sex, and the Woman Worker,* edited by Milton Cantor and Bruce Laurie. Westport, Conn.: Greenwood Press, 1977.

————. "Changing Strategies among Immigrant Generations: New York Italians in Comparative Perspective," *Journal of Social History* 15:3 (Spring 1984): 443–466.

Cremen, Lawrence. *The Transformation of the Schools: Progressivism in American Education.* New York: Knopf, 1961.

Danhof, C. H. *Change in Agriculture: The Northern United States, 1820–1970.* Cambridge, Mass.: Harvard University Press, 1969.

Davis, Kingsley and Judith Blake. "Social Structure and Fertility: An Analytical Framework," *Economic Development and Cultural Change* 4:3 (April 1956): 211–235.

DeForest, R. W. and L. Veiller. *The Tenement House Problem.* New York: MacMillan, 1903.

Demeny, Paul. "Early Fertility Decline in Austria-Hungary: A Lesson in Demographic Transition," *Daedalus* 97 (1968): 502–522.

Dublin, Thomas. *Women at Work.* New York: Columbia University Press, 1979.

Dubnoff, Steven. "The Life-Cycle and Economic Welfare: Historical Change in the Economic Constraints on Working Class Family Life, 1860–1974." Unpublished manuscript, 1978.

Easterlin, Richard A. *Population, Labor Force, and Long Swings in Economic Growth.* New York: National Bureau of Economic Research, 1968.

————. "Factors in the Decline of Farm Fertility in the United States: Some Preliminary Research Results," *Journal of American History* 63 (1976): 600–614.

————. "The Economics and Sociology of Fertility: A Synthesis." In *Historical Studies in Changing Fertility,* edited by Charles Tilly. Princeton, N.J.: Princeton University Press, 1978.

————, George Alter, and Gretchen Condran. "Farms and Farm Families in Old and New Areas: The Northern States in 1860." In *Family and Population in Nineteenth-Century America,* edited by Tamara Hareven and Maris Vinovskis. Princeton, N.J.: Princeton University Press, 1978.

Edwards, Richard. *Contested Terrain: The Transformation of the Workplace in the Twentieth Century.* New York: Basic Books, 1979.

Ehrenreich, Barbara. *The Hearts of Men: American Dreams and the Flight from Commitment.* Garden City, N.Y.: Doubleday, 1984.

Elder, Glen H., Jr. *Children of the Great Depression: Social Change in Life Experience.* Chicago: University of Chicago Press, 1974.

————. "Approaches to Social Change and the Family." In *Turning Points: Historical and Sociological Essays on the Family*, edited by John Demos and S. S. Boocock. Chicago: University of Chicago Press, 1978.

————. "Scarcity and Prosperity in Post-War Childbearing: Explanations from a Life-Course Perspective." In *The American Family in Socio-Historical Perspective*, edited by Michael Gordon. 3rd edition. New York: St. Marks, 1982.

Erlich, Richard. "The Industrial Development of Buffalo 1880 to 1900." Unpublished manuscript, 1967.

————. The Development of Buffalo, 1900 to 1967." Unpublished manuscript, 1968.

Fass, Paula. *The Damned and the Beautiful: American Youth in the 1920s*. New York: Oxford University Press, 1977.

Forster, Colin and G. S. L. Tucker. *Economic Opportunity and White Fertility Ratios*. New Haven, Conn.: Yale University Press, 1972.

Gans, Herbert. *The Urban Villagers: Group and Class in the Life of Italian-Americans*. New York: Free Press, 1962.

Gates, Paul. *The Farmer's Age: Agriculture 1815–1860*. New York: Holt, Rinehart, and Winston, 1960.

Geertz, Clifford. *The Interpretation of Culture*. New York: Basic Books, 1973.

Giddens, Anthony. *The Class Structure of the Advanced Societies*. London: Hutchinson University Library, 1973.

————. *Central Problems in Social Theory: Action, Structure, and Contradiction in Social Analysis*. Berkeley and Los Angeles: University of California Press, 1979.

————. *The Constitution of Society: An Outline of the Theory of Structuration*. Berkeley and Los Angeles: University of California Press, 1984.

Goodwin, Lawrence. *Democratic Promise: The Populist Moment in America*. New York: Oxford University Press, 1976.

Gordon, Linda. *Woman's Body, Woman's Right: A Social History of Birth Control in America*. New York: Grossman, 1976.

Green, James. *World of the Worker: Labor in Twentieth-Century America*. New York: Hill and Wang, 1980.

Greven, Peter J., Jr. *Four Generations: Population, Land, and Family in Colonial Andover, Massachusetts*. Ithaca, N.Y.: Cornell University Press, 1972.

Grabill, W. H. and Lee-Jay Cho. "Methodology for the Measurement of Current Fertility from Population Data on Young Children," *Demography* 2 (1965): 50–73.

————, C. V. Kiser, and P. K. Whelpton. *The Fertility of American Women*. New York: John Wiley and Sons, 1958.

Griffen, Clyde and Sally Griffen. *Natives and Newcomers: The Ordering of Opportunities in Mid-Nineteenth-Century Poughkeepsie*. Cambridge, Mass.: Harvard University Press, 1978.

Guest, Avery M. and Stewart Tolnay, "Urban Industrial Structure and Fertility: The Case of Large American Cities," *Journal of Interdisciplinary History* 13:3 (Winter 1983): 387–409.

Gutman, Herbert. *Society and Culture in Industrializing America*. New York: Knopf, 1976.

Handlin, Oscar. *The Uprooted*. Boston: Little, Brown, 1951.

Haines, Michael. "Poverty, Economic Stress, and the Family in a Late Nineteenth-Century City: Whites in Philadelphia, 1880." In *Philadelphia: Work, Space, Family, and Group Experience in the 19th Century*, edited by Theodore Hershberg. New York: Oxford University Press, 1981.

———. *Fertility and Occupation: Population Patterns in Industrialization*. New York: Academic Press, 1979.

———. "Recent Developments in History Demography: A Review of the European Fertility Project with Some Comparisons from Japan," *Historical Methods Newsletter* 11:4 (1979): 162–173.

Hajnal, J. "European Marriage Patterns in Perspective." In *Population in History: Essays in Historical Demography*, edited by David Glass and D.E.C. Eversley. London: Edward Arnold, 1965.

Hareven, Tamara K. *Family Time and Industrial Time*. New York: Cambridge University Press, 1982.

——— and Maris A. Vinovskis. "Marital Fertility, Ethnicity, and Occupation in Urban Families: An Analysis of South Boston and the South End in 1880," *Journal of Social History* 8 (1975): 69–93.

———. "Patterns of Childbearing in Late Nineteenth-Century America: The Determinants of Marital Fertility in Five Massachusetts Towns in 1880." In *Family and Population in Nineteenth-Century America*, edited by Tamara Hareven and Maris Vinovskis. Princeton, N.J.: Princeton University Press, 1978.

Hawthorn, Geoffrey. *The Sociology of Fertility*. London: Colliers-MacMillan, 1970.

Hays, Samuel P. "The Politics of Reform in Municipal Government in the Progressive Era," *Pacific Northwest Quarterly* 55 (October 1964): 157–169.

Henderson, J. J. *Annual Statement of the Trade and Commerce of Buffalo*. Buffalo: Board of Trade, 1855.

Hendrick, U. P. *A History of Agriculture in the State of New York*. New York: Hill and Wang, 1966 (originally published in 1933).

Henripin, Jacques. *Trends and Factors of Fertility in Canada* Ottawa: Statistics Canada, 1972.

Himes, Norman E. *Medical History of Contraception*. New York: Gamut Press, 1963.

Hogan, David John. "Education and the Making of the Chicago Working Class," *History of Education Quarterly* 18:3 (Fall 1978): 227–270.

———. *Class and Reform: School and Society in Chicago, 1880–1930*. Philadelphia: University of Pennsylvania Press, 1985.

Hofstadter, Richard. *The Age of Reform: From Bryan to FDR*. New York: Knopf, 1955.

———. *Anti-Intellectualism in American Life*. New York: Knopf, 1962.

Jerome, Harry. *Migration and the Business Cycle*. New York: National Bureau of Economic Research, 1926.

Kalecki, Michael. *Theory of Economic Dynamics*. London: Allen and Unwin, 1954.

Kantor, Harvey and David Tyack, eds. *Work, Youth, and Schooling: Historical Perspectives on Vocationalism in American Education*. Stanford, Ca.: Stanford University Press, 1982.

Karier, Clarence. *Shaping the American Educational State.* New York: Free Press, 1973.

Katz, Michael B. *The Irony of Early School Reform.* Cambridge, Mass.: Harvard University Press, 1967.

————. *The People of Hamilton, Canada West: Class and Family in a Mid-Nineteenth Century City.* Cambridge, Mass.: Harvard University Press, 1975.

————. "The Origins of Public Education: A Reassessment," *History of Education Quarterly* 16:1 (Winter 1976): 381–407.

———— and Ian E. Davey. "Youth and Early Industrialization in a Canadian City." In *Turning Points: Historical and Sociological Essays on the Family,* edited by John Demos and S. S. Boocock. Chicago: University of Chicago Press, 1978.

————, Michael J. Doucet, and Mark J. Stern. *The Social Organization of Early Industrial Capitalism.* Cambridge, Mass.: Harvard University Press, 1982.

———— and Mark J. Stern. "Fertility, Class, and Industrial Capitalism: Erie County, New York, 1855–1915," *American Quarterly* 33:1 (Spring 1981): 63–92.

Keyssar, Alexander. *Out of Work: The First Century of Unemployment in Massachusetts.* Cambridge: Cambridge University Press, 1986.

Kennedy, David M. *Birth Control in America: The Career of Margaret Sanger.* New Haven, Conn.: Yale University Press, 1970.

Kett, Joseph. *Rites of Passage: Adolescence in America, 1790 to the Present.* New York: Basic Books, 1977.

Kilduff, R. "Social Buffalo: A Working Community?" Unpublished manuscript, n.d.

Kiser, C. V., W. H. Grabill, and A. A. Campbell. *Trends and Variations in Fertility in the United States.* Cambridge, Mass.: Harvard University Press, 1968.

Knodel, John E. *The Decline of Fertility in Germany, 1871–1939.* Princeton, N.J.: Princeton University Press, 1974.

———— and E. van de Walle. "Lessons from the Past: Policy Implications of Historical Fertility Studies," *Population and Development Review* 5:2 (June 1979): 217–245.

Kolko, Gabriel. *Main Currents in Modern American History.* New York: Harper and Row, 1976.

Kuhn, Thomas S. *The Structure of Scientific Revolutions.* 2nd Edition. Chicago: University of Chicago, 1970.

Lasch, Christopher. *Haven in a Heartless World: The Family Besieged.* New York: Basic Books, 1977.

Landes, David S. *The Unbound Prometheus: Technological Change and Industrial Development in Western Europe from 1750 to the Present.* Cambridge: Cambridge University Press, 1972.

Lazerson, Marvin. *Origins of the Urban School.* Cambridge, Mass.: Harvard University Press, 1971.

Lear, T. Jackson. "The Concept of Cultural Hegemony: Problems and Possibilities," *American Historical Review* 90:3 (June 1985): 567–593.

Leet, D. R. "Human Fertility and Agricultural Opportunities in Ohio Counties: From Frontier to Maturity, 1810–1860." in *Essays in Nineteenth Century Economic*

History: The Old Northwest, edited by D. C. Kingaman and R. K. Vedder. Athens, Ohio: Ohio University Press, 1975.

Lesthaeghe, Ron. "On the Social Control of Human Reproduction," *Population and Development Review* 6:4 (December 1980): 527–548.

——— and Chris Wilson. "The Fertility Decline in Western Europe, 1870–1930." Unpublished manuscript.

Leuchtenberg, William. *The Perils of Prosperity, 1914–1932*. Chicago: University of Chicago Press, 1958.

Levy, Sidney. "The Grain Scoopers of Buffalo: An Essay in Local Labor History." Master's thesis, University of Buffalo, 1940.

Lindert, Peter H. *Fertility and Scarcity in America*. Princeton, N.J.: Princeton University Press, 1978.

Livi Bracci, Massimo. *A Century of Portuguese Fertility*. Princeton, N.J.: Princeton University Press, 1971.

Lynd, Robert S. and Helen M. Lynd. *Middletown: A Study in Modern American Culture*. New York: Harcourt, Brace, and World, 1929.

MacDonagh, Oliver "The Irish Famine Emigration to the United States," *Perspectives in American History*, 10 (1976): 357–448.

McLaren, Angus. *Birth Control in Nineteenth Century England*. New York: Holmes and Meier, 1978.

Matthews, Fred. "Hobbesian Populism: Interpretive Paradigms and Moral Vision in American Historiography," *Journal of American History* 72:1 (June 1985): 92–115.

Meyer, Stephen, III. *The Five-Dollar Day: Labor Management and Social Control in the Ford Motor Company, 1908–1921*. Albany, N.Y.: State University of New York Press, 1981.

Mills, C. Wright. *White Collar: The American Middle Classes*. New York: Oxford University Press, 1951.

Modell, John, "Family and Fertility on the Indiana Frontier, 1820," *American Quarterly* 23 (1971): 615–634.

———. "Patterns of Consumption, Acculturation, and Family Income Strategies in Late 19th-Century America. In *Family and Population in Nineteenth-Century America*, edited by Tamara Hareven and Maris Vinovskis. Princeton, N.J.: Princeton University Press, 1978.

———, Frank Furstenberg, and Theodore Hershberg. "Social Change and Transitions to Adulthood in Historical Perspective." In *Philadelphia: Work, Space, Family, and Group Experience in the 19th Century*, edited by Theodore Hershberg. New York: Oxford University Press, 1981.

——— and Tamara Hareven. "Urbanization and the Malleable Household: An Examination of Boarding and Lodging in American Families," *Journal of Marriage and the Family* 35 (August 1973): 467–478.

Mohr, James. *Abortion in America: The Origins and Evolution of National Policy*. New York: Oxford University Press, 1978.

Musgrove, Floyd. *Youth and the Social Order*. Bloomington, Ind.: Indiana University Press, 1964.

Noble, David. *America by Design: Science, Technology, and the Rise of Corporate Capitalism.* New York: Oxford University Press, 1977.

Notestein, Frank W. "Economic Problems of Population Change," *Proceedings of the Eighth International Conference of Agricultural Economists.* London: Oxford University Press, 1953.

Ornati, Oscar. *Poverty Amid Affluence.* New York: Twentieth Century Fund, 1966.

Osterman, Paul. *Getting Started: The Youth Labor Market.* Cambridge, Mass.: MIT Press, 1980.

Perlmann, A. J. "Education and the Social Structure of an American City." Unpublished Ph.D. dissertation, Harvard University, 1980.

Piore, Michael J. *Birds of Passage: Migrant Labor and Industrial Societies.* New York: Cambridge University Press, 1979.

Rainwater, Lee. *And the Poor Get Children: Sex, Contraception, and Family Planning in the Working Class.* Chicago: Quadrangle Books, 1960.

Ranum, O. and P. Ranum, eds. *Popular Attitudes toward Birth Control in Pre-Industrial France and England.* New York: Harper and Row, 1972.

Ravitch, Diane. *Revisionist Revised: A Critique of the Radical Attack on the Schools.* New York: Basic Books, 1978.

Reed, James. *From Private Vice to Public Virtue: The Birth Control Movement and American Society Since 1830.* New York: Basic Books, 1978.

Rodgers, Daniels T. *The Work Ethic in Industrial America, 1850–1920.* Chicago: University of Chicago Press, 1978.

Schnittman, Suzanne G. "Irregular Employment in Buffalo, New York from 1870 to 1971." Master's thesis, State University of New York at Brockport, 1979.

Schumpeter, Joseph. *Capitalism, Socialism, and Democracy* New York: Harper and Row, 1950.

Shergold, Peter R. *Working Class Life: The "American Standard" in Comparative Perspective, 1899–1913.* Pittsburgh: University of Pittsburgh Press, 1982.

Sellers, Maxine S. *Ethnic Communities and Education in Buffalo, New York: Politics, Power, and Group Identity, 1830–1979.* Buffalo: State University of New York at Buffalo, 1979.

Shorter, Edward. "Female Emancipation, Birth Control, and Fertility in European History," *American Historical Review* 78 (1973): 605–633.

———. *The Making of the Modern Family.* London: Collins, 1976.

Stack, Carol. *All Our Kin: Strategies for Survival in a Black Community.* New York: Harper and Row, 1974.

Stedman Jones, Gareth. *Outcast London: A Study in the Relationship between Classes in Victorian Society.* Oxford: Clarendon Press, 1971.

———. "Working Class Culture and Working Class Politics in London, 1870–1900: Notes on the Remaking of a Working Class," *Journal of Social History* 7:4 (Summer 1974): 460–508.

Steindl, Joseph. *Maturity and Stagnation in American Capitalism.* Oxford: Blackwell, 1952.

Stern, Mark J. "The Demography of Capitalism: Industry, Class, and Fertility in Erie County, New York, 1855–1915," Ph.D. dissertation, York University, 1979.

Sullivan, J. M. "Models for the Estimation of the Probability of Dying between Birth and Exact Ages in Early Childhood," *Population Studies* 26:1 (April 1972): 79–97.

Synge, Jane. "The Transition from School to Work: Working-Class Adolescence in Early 20th Century Hamilton." Unpublish manuscript, n.d.

Tabbarah, R. B. "Birth Control and Population Policy," *Population Studies* 18 (1964): 187–196.

———. "Toward a Theory of Demographic Development," *Economic Development and Cultural Change* 19 (1971): 257–277.

Thernstrom, Stephan. *The Other Bostonians: Poverty and Progress in the American Metropolis*. Cambridge, Mass.: Harvard University Press, 1973.

Thomas, W. I. and F. Znaniecki. *The Polish Peasant in Europe and America*. 2 vol. Chicago: University of Chicago Press, 1918–1920.

Thompson, Edward P. *The Making of the English Working Class*. New York: Vintage Books, 1963.

Thompson, W. and P. K. Whelpton. *Population Trends in the United States*. New York: McGraw Hill, 1933.

Thurstone, William. *Statement of the Trade and Commerce of Buffalo*. Buffalo: Board of Trade, 1870.

———. *Statistics and Information Relative to the Trade and Commerce of Buffalo*. Buffalo: Board of Trade, 1874.

Tilly, Charles. "The Historical Study of Vital Processes." In *Historical Studies of Changing Fertility*, edited by Charles Tilly. Princeton, N.J.: Princeton University Press, 1978.

Tilly, Louise A. and Joan W. Scott. *Women, Work, and Family*. New York: Holt, Rinehart, and Winston, 1978.

Tolnay, Stuart E., Stephan N. Graham, and Avery M. Guest. "Own-Child Estimates of U.S. White Fertility, 1886–1900," *Historical Methods* 15:3 (Summer 1982): 127–138.

Trachtenberg, Alan. *The Incorporation of America: Culture and Society in the Gilded Age*. New York: Hill and Wang, 1982.

Trussel, T. J. "A Re-estimation of the Multiplying Factors for the Brass Technique for Determining Childhood Survivorship Rates," *Population Studies* 29:1 (April 1975): 97–107.

United States, Census, Bureau of the. *Manufactures of the United States, 1860*. Washington, D.C.: Government Printing Office, 1865.

———. Nineth Census. *Industry and Wealth*. Washington, D.C.: Government Printing Office, 1875.

———. *Report on the Manufactures of the United States at the Tenth Census*. Washington, D.C.: Government Printing Office, 1883.

———. Eleventh Census. *Census of Manufactures. Part II. Report on Cities*. Washington, D.C.: Government Printing Office, 1895.

————. Twelfth Census. Volume 8. *Manufactures*. Washington, D.C.: Government Printing Office, 1900.

————. Census of Manufactures. 1914. Volume I. *Report by States with Statistics for Principal Cities and Metropolitan Districts*. Washington, D.C.: Government Printing Office, 1918.

————. Sixteenth Census. *Differential Fertility 1910–1940*. Washington, D.C.: Government Printing Office, 1945.

United States, Labor, Department of. Bureau of Labor Statistics. *Cost of Living in the United States*. Bulletin #357. Washington, D.C.: Government Printing Office, 1924.

van de Walle, Etienne. *The Female Population of France in the Nineteenth Century: A Reconstitution of 82 Departements*. Princeton, N.J.: Princeton University Press, 1974.

———— and John Knodel. "Demographic Transition and Fertility Decline: The European Case." Sidney: International Union for the Scientific Study of Population, 1967.

————. "Europe's Fertility Transition: New Evidence and Lessons for Today's Developing World," *Population Bulletin* 34:6 (February 1980): 3–43.

Veblen, T. *The Theory of the Leisure Class*. New York, 1899.

Vinovskis, Maris A. "Socio-economic Determinants of Interstate Fertility Differentials in the United States in 1850 and 1860," *Journal of Interdisciplinary History* 6 (1976): 781–786.

————. "A Multivariate Regression Analysis of Fertility Differentials among Massachusetts Regions and Towns in 1860." In *Historical Studies in Changing Fertility*, edited by Charles Tilly. Princeton, N.J.: Princeton University Press, 1978.

————. *Fertility in Massachusetts from the Revolution to the Civil War*. New York: Academic Press, 1981.

Walkowitz, Daniel J. *Worker City, Company Town: Iron and Cotton Worker Protest in Troy and Cohoe, New York, 1855–1884*. Urbana: University of Illinois, 1978.

Wallace, Anthony F. C. *Rockdale: The Growth of an American Village in the Early Industrial Revolution*. New York: Norton, 1980.

Wiebe, Robert H. *The Search for Order, 1877–1920*. New York: Hill and Wang, 1967.

Wrigley, E. A. "Family Limitation in Pre-Industrial England," *Economic History Review*. 2nd series. 29 (April 1966): 82–109.

Yans McLaughlin, Virginia. "Patterns of Work and Family Organization: Buffalo's Italians." In *The Family in History: Interdisciplinary Essays*, edited by T. K. Rabb and R. I. Rotberg. New York: Harper and Row, 1971.

————. *Family and Community: Italian Immigrants in Buffalo, 1880–1930*. Ithaca: Cornell University Press, 1977.

Yasuba, Yasukichi. *Birth Rates of the White Population in the United States, 1800–1860*. Baltimore: Johns Hopkins Press, 1962.

Young, Michael and Peter Wilmot. *Family and Kinship in East London*. Hammondsworth, Eng.: Penguin Books, 1962.

Zelizer, Viviana A.*Pricing the Priceless Child: The Changing Value of Children*. New York: Basic Books, 1985.

Zimmerman, C. C. *Consumption and Standards of Living*. New York: VanNostrand, 1936.

Zunz, Olivier. *The Changing Face of Inequality: Urbanization, Industrial Development and Immigrants in Detroit, 1880–1920*. Chicago: University of Chicago Press, 1982.

Index

Adams, J.N.: mayor of Buffalo, 32
Alter, George: with George Easterlin, and Gretchen Condran, and the land availability thesis, 8–9, 118
Automobile industry: Buffalo, 28–29

Banks, J.A.: England, fertility decline in, 73–74
Bash, Wendell: study of fertility in Madison County, New York, 116–117
Birth spacing: and family limitation, 58–59
Birthplace: as determinant of fertility, 120
Birthrate: and fertility, 55–57
Blake, Judith, 93
Boarding: and working class, 42
British immigrants: see Immigrants
Buffalo: Economic and social development of, 1850–1920, 23–45; population characteristics of, 33–36; urban problems of, 30–31; Chamber of Commerce, 31–32
Business Class: in Buffalo, 30–33, 36–39; in Erie County, 51–55; family strategy of, 71–74

Caldwell, John: as education relates to fertility, 17, 109–114, 130; theory of fertility decline, 13–22, 73, 93–95, 130
Canadian immigrants: see Immigrants

Child labor: and working class, 42
Clerks: changing occupational position, 38
Coale, Ansley: Director of the European Fertility Project, 13–14; "m statistic", with Trussel, 18, 59; and Trussel, age structure of marital fertility, 59
Cohen, Miriam: Italian and Jewish families in New York City, 97–99; criticism of Yans-McLaughlin
Condran, Gretchen: with George Easterlin and George Alter and the land availability thesis, 8–9, 118
Control of fertility: attempts made, 58–70
Cubberley, Judith: 96
Cremin, Lawrence: 96
Culture: and fertility, 19–20, 70, 77–78, 133

Demographic transition, theory of: Frank Notestein, formulator 12–14
Doucet, Michael: with Michael Katz and Mark Stern, analysis of nineteenth century Hamilton and Buffalo, 16–17; *The Social Organization of Early Industrial Capitalism*, 50–55, 85, 131–132
Dubnoff, Steven: 74
Dupont Chemical: acquires German patents, 28
Dyes: in Buffalo, 28